SISTERS

... no way!

Ashling's Diary

Siobhán Parkinson

THE O'BRIEN PRESS
DUBLIN

First published 1996 by The O'Brien Press Ltd,
20 Victoria Road, Dublin 6, Ireland.
Tel: +353 1 4923333; Fax: +353 1 4922777
E-mail: books@obrien.ie
Website: www.obrien.ie
Reprinted 1997 (twice), 1998, 1999, 2002, 2005.

ISBN 0-86278-495-6

British Library Cataloguing-in-Publication Data
Parkinson, Siobhan
Sisters
1. Children's stories, English
I. Title
823.9'14 [J]

7 8 9 10 11
05 06 07 08 09

The O'Brien Press receives
assistance from

Typesetting, layout, editing, design: The O'Brien Press Ltd
Printing: Cox & Wyman Ltd

Cover photographs courtesy of Corbis

SISTERS
... no way!

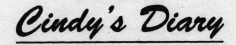
Cindy's Diary

Siobhán Parkinson

THE O'BRIEN PRESS
DUBLIN

First published 1996 by The O'Brien Press Ltd,
20 Victoria Road, Dublin 6, Ireland.
Tel: +353 1 4923333; Fax: +353 1 4922777
E-mail: books@obrien.ie
Website: www.obrien.ie
Reprinted 1997 (twice), 1998, 1999, 2002, 2005.

ISBN 0-86278-495-6

British Library Cataloguing-in-Publication Data
Parkinson, Siobhan
Sisters
1. Children's stories, English
I. Title
823.9'14 [J]

7 8 9 10 11
05 06 07 08 09

The O'Brien Press receives
assistance from

Typesetting, layout, editing, design: The O'Brien Press Ltd
Printing: Cox & Wyman Ltd

Cover photographs courtesy of Corbis

We always laugh about Gavin's birthday being on April Fool's Day, but it's not much of a consolation really. Gavin is a very sweet child, and it's not his fault that his birth, his very existence, sealed our fate. We sent him a card. We always do. I think it was sealed anyway – our fate I mean, not the card, a sealed card costs fourpence more to post – but Alva used to have a desperate hope, until Gavin was born. Then even she had to start to see that we weren't all going to live happily ever after.

That's why she cries in the night, like last night. She usually sleeps with the door open, but when she wants to have a weep, she creeps out of bed and closes her door. That always puts me on the alert. I can hear the creak as she gets out of bed, then her footsteps padding across the carpet, and the soft click as the lock engages. I don't hear the creak as she gets back into bed, presumably because the door is closed, but within minutes I can hear her sobs coming through the wall. She always cries rhythmically, so you can predict each gasp. I lie there, tense, listening for each one. I daren't go to her. I know she's embarrassed about it. Otherwise she wouldn't close the door.

It's heartbreaking. All I can do is lie there and listen to it, and will her to drift off to sleep. When the gaps between the sobs get longer, I know she is getting sleepy, and it will soon stop.

It's been going on for four years now. It was worse in the beginning. Then she was only nine. At first she did it to make Mum come, but then later, when she was past the stage of loud hysterical shrieks and screams, I think she started to use quiet tears as a punishment, to make Mum feel guilty. There is a sly side to Alva. I don't blame her. It's hard to lose your father when

3

you're only nine. It makes you distrustful.

I lost him too, of course, but I was older. Not that much older – some people would say twelve is an even worse age – but I was quite a grown-up twelve, I suppose, and I wasn't Daddy's favourite. Alva adored him, ever since she was a tiny little thing. I remember her in her high chair, waving her stubby little arms and legs, her whole body going into a paroxysm of delight when he came home in the evenings.

Mum would be feeding her her tea, but as soon as Daddy appeared Alva would start to push the spoon aside impatiently, her fat little fingers all splayed like a starfish. I remember that once she splattered baby rice all over Mum's blouse. Nothing would do her then until Dad put down his briefcase and came and fed her himself. He used to play little games with her, holding the spoon of food away out of her reach, and she would be laughing and sizzling with anticipation and excitement and banging on the tray of the high chair, and then he would swoop the spoon at high speed and accompanied by aeroplane noises, or bus noises, or motorbike noises – every spoonful got a different noise, that was part of the fun – wham into her wide-open, pink-rimmed, pulsating little mouth.

After she'd eaten up all her tea, Daddy would swoop her out of the high chair and throw her up at the ceiling. Mum used to say she would bring up all her food if he jostled her around like that, but she never did. She was always vomiting all over Mum, but she never once as much as dribbled on Dad that I can remember. I would sit in my corner – I had a little table of my own, for eating off and playing at, I think it might have been an old school desk – and watch them. After a while he might remember I was there and come over with the baby wriggling delightedly under his arm and put his hand on my head and say something sweet and meaningless. I usually didn't answer, just looked at him solemnly and went on cutting up my French toast. Sometimes Mum would come and sit beside me, crouching down to my level, and ask if I would like jam. I always loved her for that. It seemed to me such an entirely relevant question, and one I could answer, instead of, And what did Daddy's little poppet learn at playschool today?

It wasn't a case of me and Mum against Dad and Alva or anything like that. I loved him too. It was just that she and he had a very special closeness. He used to take her fishing. I wasn't jealous. He asked me to come fishing lots of times too, but I was afraid of seeing the fish dying. I think I was even more afraid of the idea that they might not die, and he would have to kill them. I didn't want to see him killing the fish. Alva didn't have to see him doing that, because she did it herself. You just catch them by the tail, she said, and give their head a good wallop on the ground. But I couldn't imagine catching a fish by the tail. Surely it would slither out of your hand – wouldn't it be all slimy and hard to get a grip on? And your hand, wouldn't it smell fishy afterwards? So instead I would stay at home with Mum, and we would make a coating for the fish. Sometimes we used just flour with pepper and salt in it. Sometimes we made a more elaborate batter with egg and breadcrumbs. Once or twice we even used cornflakes. You have to put the cornflakes in a plastic bag and then roll them with a rolling pin to crush them. I liked that. I liked the sensation of rolling the bag and feeling the cornflakes scrunching under the rolling pin, but I didn't like the taste. The combination of fish and cornflakes always seemed incongruous to me.

It's usually on the nights after we come home from his place that she cries herself to sleep. We go there for visits every now and then. It used to be every second weekend when we were younger, then it became once a month, and now it's really only token visits, two or three times a year. He likes to show us off when we're with him. He takes us around and introduces us to people he knows, My daughters, from before, you know.

I don't like being a daughter from before. It's almost like he's saying we're girls he sees sometimes because we used to be his daughters. I don't like it, but Alva finds it unbearable, to go from being the light of his life, the apple of his eye, his fairy princess, his angel-cherub, to being one of his daughters from before. It kills her, and when we come home she weeps for nights on end. She never talks about him now, between visits, but she used to all the time. She was for ever planning things, working out dramatic scenarios in her head, staging events, in which she was the star, and he was the male lead. She would work it all out, and then she would tell me the story, like the plot of a film she'd seen. These dramas all took different twists, but they always had the same ending: Daddy would come home and he and Mum would be married again, and it would all go on as before. Of course it never happened. It couldn't happen, but she couldn't see that at the time, not at the age of nine. It just wasn't on, and especially not after Gavin was born.

Friday 4th April

Alva and I are going to paint her bedroom this weekend. I said I would buy the paint, instead of an Easter egg this year. I thought it would cheer her up.

I got Mum to leave us at the DIY shop yesterday, while she went off with her trolley in that distracted way of hers – she goes into a complete trance once she enters a supermarket, I don't know why – and we chose the paint. It's a very, very pale pink, so pale you could almost call it white.

The best part is that it was on special offer, so it didn't cost a fortune. I love getting things cheap. Money is a bit of a problem in our house. Mum's job is only part-time. In some jobs, part-time is fine, because you can get by on half a salary if you really put your mind to it and anyway you pay less tax, but Mum is a teacher, which means that there are three months in the summer, plus other holidays, when she doesn't get paid at all, so cash is always tight with us.

Dad pays our school fees. That's his contribution to the family economy, that and half the mortgage. He says he doesn't agree with single-sex education. The only mixed school in our area is a fee-paying one, but he insisted we go there anyway. I don't really believe it has anything to do with co-education. I think it's just snobbery, but I love our school, so I don't argue. That's the only extravagant thing about our lives. We are always having to plan our finances and budget for things.

I help Mum with all that side of things. She's not very good with figures, but we do it together and it's very satisfying, seeing the columns all adding up and balancing out. I've got her into the habit of using her credit card for most things, and we only keep enough cash for bread and milk and the paper, so we don't buy things we haven't planned for, like expensive magazines or sudden-impulse takeaways. We have an emergency fiver, in the bottom of a spaghetti jar – one of those long ones, so it's hard to get it out unless you really need it.

Alva is delighted with her bedroom. She gave me a big painty hug and half-smothered me in kisses on Sunday when we finished it and said I was the best big sister anybody ever had and that nobody ever had such a brillo bedroom ever ever before. It is nice, I must say, not too pink, just a nice soft rosy glow. She tore up all the old posters and pin-ups and postcards she'd had festooned over her walls, saying that they were all too raggy and dog-eared for such a beautiful room, and she went out and bought an enormous, shiny technicolour poster of Boyzone and put it up reverently with blu-tack. Mum and I had to act as consultants while she put it up, and she kept begging us to tell her whether it was properly centred and whether it would be in a glare when the curtains were open. At one point she even wished she had Dad's spirit level so she could be completely sure it was straight. Dad took all his DIY tools with him, which was a bit mean of him. We never have a hammer or a pliers or anything.

When the poster was exactly where Alva wanted it, Mum and I had to stand there and admire it, nudging each other secretly, and agreeing that the lads were just the pinnacle of male desirability. So there they are, like Matthew, Mark, Luke and John and a stray friend blessing the bed that she lies on, and grinning down with their toothpasty smiles at her all night long. I suppose they are quite goodlooking, really, if you're going on fourteen.

I wish it was as easy to cheer Mum up. She's never been the same since Dad left. I know that's natural, up to a point, but I think it's time she started picking up the pieces and making a new life for herself. It's all very well for us, I tell her, we'll get over it in our own way, and we'll go on and leave school and get jobs and maybe get married, but she could just get stuck at this point in her life. I keep telling her that she should be going out to clubs for separated people and finding some nice man who will be kind to her. She just laughs when I say that. I think she thinks there aren't any kind men. But that can't be so. Bob is kind, for example, as well as being cute.

It's not as though she's going to meet anyone through her work. She teaches in a convent school. Actually, she doesn't really teach much. She specialises in guidance counselling nowadays, which is more one-to-one sort of work, and she only does a few hours a week in the classroom. She's interested in helping people with their career choices, and she says she feels she has a special empathy with teenage girls who are going through family difficulties, and she likes to be able to help them in any way she can. (I don't think she realises Alva cries herself to sleep.) She's very earnest about her work, takes it very seriously, and she's always reading American books about self-development. I'm a bit dubious about self-development. I can't help thinking it's just a buzz-word for selfishness, but she seems to find it interesting, and in her case, it's not her own self-development she is thinking about, but the self-development of 'her' girls.

It's all girls in the school she teaches in, and there are only two male teachers, both about twenty-two, which is not very promising for somebody like Mum, not like working in a glamorous job like television or publishing or something like that, where I am sure there are lots of interesting, kind, middle-aged men, just what Mum needs.

Mum seemed more distracted than usual today. It was my turn to cook. During the week, we take it in turns to cook dinner, so everyone does it twice a week and the two who don't cook do the washing up. We just have very quick, simple, cheap things like pasta or an omelet or a really thick vegetable soup or maybe sausages and mash. Then on Sundays we have a proper Sunday lunch and we all cook it together, a joint venture we call it. That's a joke, because we usually have a joint of meat, our only real meat meal of the week, and we all do it together, jointly.

Alva and I wash up on Sundays, to give Mum a day off from the sink. Alva moans about this, because *she* never gets Sundays off from the sink, but I am firm with her on this one. Mum needs the break more than we do. She has a tough time with school and everything. That argument doesn't impress Alva, who thinks nobody could find life as tough as she does, and she has the nerve to argue that since Mum only does school part-time and we do it full-time, we are the ones who should get Sunday off from washing up. Sometimes I worry that Alva will grow up without any sense of empathy with other people. I will lay the blame at Dad's door if she does.

Anyway, I was talking about Mum. She came into the kitchen just as I was putting a quiche in the oven, and she slumped into one of the kitchen chairs. She didn't say anything, which is a sure sign that she is preoccupied, because she usually sniffs the air and tries to guess what you're cooking or she offers to help. A couple of times I have had to forcibly steer her away from the cooker on Alva's days and frogmarch her to the kitchen table, insisting that Alva is big enough and competent enough to do it herself, but also lazy enough to let someone else take it on.

I asked her what was bothering her, but she said it was just a girl she'd had that day at school, somebody she described as 'very distressed'. Mum is always discreet about her clients, as she calls them, the girls she counsels. She confines herself to general remarks. I asked if the girl was being abused. Mum said no, nothing like that, she had been bereaved and was reacting badly, being smart with teachers at school, attention-seeking tactics, that sort of thing. Poor girl, whoever she is. Mum takes these things to heart. I'm sure she's a really great counsellor, for the people she works with, but it wears her down sometimes. She's too kind-hearted for her own good.

Tuesday 22nd April

Mum was on the phone for ages yesterday. I was getting a bit edgy, because I wanted to practise, and I can't when someone's on the phone. I play the double-bass, and when I'm practising, the whole house vibrates. We've had to apologise to the neighbours – we live in a semi and the walls are not the most sound-proof – and we've agreed that I will only practise between five and six in the evenings. Alva plays the flute. Nobody minds a flute, no matter when it's played. That's typical of Alva. Everything she does is fine with everyone. I'm the one that has to tiptoe around, trying not to offend people, smoothing things over all the time. Sometimes I wish I was the youngest for a change.

Anyway, Mum made a phone call just as I was about to get out my bow, and she was on for ages. I waited and waited until at last she hung up. I only got about fifteen minutes of practice in before I heard the angelus bell on the kitchen radio and knew I had to stop. It's not like Mum, so it must have been quite an important phone call. Probably something to do with school.

Thursday 1st May

Mum was out last night. She doesn't usually go out mid-week, but she said it was a parent–teacher meeting. I didn't think they had parent–teacher meetings in May, but she said this was a special one she had arranged with a particular parent. She's far too dedicated to that job.

Bob came over to celebrate Bealtaine. He is interested pagan festivals. I should explain that Bob is my boyfriend. His mother calls him Robert. I call him Bob. It started out sort of like a petname, but now Mum and Alva and all my friends call him that too. He's in sixth year. I've been going out with him for a few months now. He's very cute, and he's fun to be with. He's tall and his profile is rather chiselled. It's his noble nose that does it, I think, and his smooth forehead. Mum thinks he's a bit wild, because he drinks. I told her everyone in sixth year drinks, even the girls, which is an understatement, and anyway he only drinks beer, he doesn't get drunk, much, and he doesn't smoke. Smoke! screeched my mother when I mentioned this word. I meant tobacco, but she made it sound as if I was talking about heroin. As if I would have anything to do with anybody who did stuff like that! Honestly, when I think how hard I try to understand Mum, I think she might make an effort to understand me too. I said he *doesn't* smoke, I repeated, but I think even mentioning the word smoke in connection with Bob was enough to make Mum suspicious. She's a bit over-protective, but once she got to know Bob she settled down. He's very good at handling parents. Talks about choosing the right subjects for the Leaving and how the points system works and stuff like that. (I take back the bit about Mum not making an effort to understand me. She's a great mother really. I must try not to be Alva-ish.)

Anyway, Bob and I made a sort of punch in the kitchen, consisting of heated up honey, diluted with some orange juice (out of a packet) and lemon juice (out of a lemon) and a shot of vodka. Neither of us drinks spirits normally, so we only used a tiny drop of vodka, just so it would be realistic, because we were pretending it was mead. We poured it into a sort of squat little vase thing we found under the sink, because it had handles, and we wanted something we could both hold. We called it a loving cup and we drank to each other's health and fertility. I was a bit worried about the fertility part, tempting fate I thought, but Bob said that was the sort of thing the Celts drank to, so I did. There was hardly any alcohol in it, and it tasted pretty disgusting, which may have had something to do with the fact that we had to scrub out the loving cup with Jif, because it was caked with dust.

Alva heard us laughing in the kitchen and came in and said she wanted some mead too. We had a job persuading her that that wouldn't be a good idea. When we said she couldn't have any because there was vodka in it, she said, Ooh, I'm telling! as if we were little kids. I'm sorry I told her about the vodka now, not because I think she'll 'tell' – I don't care if she does – but because I think it might have given her the wrong idea. She might think drinking vodka at sixteen is OK , which I don't really think it is. It was only a tiny drop, and we only added it in for authenticity, but now I feel we shouldn't have. It's no joke being an older sister, especially if your younger sister is a bit on the impressionable side, like Alva. It's a terrible responsibility. If you didn't watch her, she'd be swigging neat vodka in no time at all and topping the bottle up with water. I'm not exaggering. They do that sort of thing, you know, in her class, and that's the normal ones. The rest are anorexic and don't eat, not to mind drink. It's an awful age. But they can't help it. It's their hormones.

I managed to get her to bed before half-past ten, which was something, I suppose. Bob left soon after that, and I went to bed myself. I didn't hear Mum come in. It must have been late.

Sunday 4th May

Mum was on the phone again this morning, another long session. I was just basting the chicken when she came back into the kitchen and it was sizzling noisily, so I had to wait until I'd got it back in the oven. Then I straightened up and said, Well, whoever it is, it must be somebody interesting.

Whoever who is? she asked.

Whoever all these mysterious phone calls are to, I said, smiling encouragement.

She went bright red and started to flap her hands in front of her face to cool herself down. It's hot in here, she said.

Oven, I replied. But I wasn't going to let her get off that easily. Well? I said.

It's none of your business, she replied.

I shrugged nonchalantly. I didn't push it, partly because I respect her privacy, but partly because I thought there was a better chance of her telling me eventually if I didn't try to worm it out of her. I hope that isn't very devious of me. I have her best interests at heart. I hope it's a man. I know that's very conventional of me, but there you go. I can't help it.

Thursday 8th May

Mum was out again last night. Another mid-week appointment. Hm! Bob thinks I should ask her straight out if I am so concerned. I'm not *concerned*, I told him, just interested. But I am concerned really, and curious.

Sunday 11th May

Alva announced yesterday that she was going to a rave. We were just home from the supermarket, and we were unpacking the bags. At least, Mum and I were unpacking them and Alva was opening the chocolate biscuits, which was her idea of contributing to the domestic chores. A rave? said Mum. Sounds fun! Really, sometimes Mum is so vague it would drive you up the wall. She knows perfectly well what goes on at raves, but she has these little plastic containers she keeps in the fridge, labelled Sausages, Rashers, Cheese, and I could see she was wondering which one to put the salami she had bought 'for a change' into. I know she would happily have run out and bought another little plastic box and labelled it Salami, if I hadn't been there to prevent her, just to solve the problem, rather than put salami in a box labelled Rashers.

You're not going to a rave, Alva, I said. That was a bit bossy of me, I know, but it was clear that Mum wasn't going to say it. Did I say she can be a bit vague sometimes?

I am so, she said, biting savagely into a chocolate biscuit. Everyone's going.

The first biscuit out of a newly opened packet of chocolate digestives is always extremely fresh. There were biscuit crumbs everywhere.

Who precisely is everyone? asked Mum, her parent-of-a-teenager skills suddenly kicking in.

Raves are out anyway, I added. I know that because I read it somewhere, but I said it as if I knew it from personal experience.

You just don't understand! Alva shouted, and tore out of the room. We could hear the fast and furious pounding of her shoes on the stairs.

Mum and I exchanged glances, meaning we do understand, all too well. I felt we were not a mother and daughter, just two women shaking our heads about a child.

Put it just loose in the fridge, in its bag, I said, if you really can't make up your mind.

Good idea, Ashling, she said. You really are such a support to me, love.

I felt quite overcome. A sort of a warm wave of love and gratitude washed over me. I knew she didn't mean just about the salami.

I'd better go and try to get some sense out of her, she went on.

Sooner you than me, I said. I'll make a pot of tea. It'll be ready for you when you come down.

She shot me one of her radiant smiles from the door. She is not a particularly beautiful woman, but her smile is like the sun coming out.

Mum and Alva came down together. The tea was cold. I'll make a fresh pot, I said. Alva's face was mottled from crying. I was dying to ask what had been said. I can guess anyway. Mum probably asked her again just who was going to this rave and where it was being held and what time it was over at and whether she had a lift home, and Alva probably got so upset at the questions that she decided to drop the whole thing. That must be roughly what happened anyway, because the subject wasn't raised again, and Alva didn't go anywhere last night.

Saturday 17th May

I took Alva shopping today, to make up for being hard on her last week about the rave. It was her birthday on Wednesday, and she had some birthday money that Dad sent her, burning a hole in her pocket. So I took some money out of my post office account and we went off into town, to treat ourselves. We weren't really planning to buy anything. Only if we saw something we really liked.

There's a bargain shop I know about, where they sell out-of-season clothes, so we went there just to have a look. Sometimes the things are nice, but most of the time the stuff is creased and weary looking, and in dreadful colours you wouldn't be seen dead in. But today they had some irresistible knife-pleated skirts, very short. I tried one on, and it looked great. I have good legs, even if I say so myself, especially in black tights, and short skirts suit me. I usually buy my clothes in Penney's or somewhere like that. I never had a really good wool skirt before, but this was only fifteen pounds. It's a green tartan. Alva thought it was lovely, and even though she never wears skirts except at school, she decided she'd get one too, so she tried a navy tartan, and it looked great on her.

We look just like sisters, I said, joking.

We are sisters, she said, puzzled.

She doesn't really have a great sense of humour. Anyway, the skirts were great value, and with Irish summers what they are we'll probably get to wear them most of the year around. Alva wanted to wear hers straight away, but I said it would get ruined on the bus, and anyway she didn't have any tights, and it would look a

17

bit silly with bare legs and an old pair of black socks with bobbles on them from washing, so I got her to agree to have it folded up in tissue paper and put in a paper carrier bag. They have anonymous brown paper bags in this shop, with paper handles, which I think are quite smart.

Then we went to a coffee shop, one of those trendy new places in Temple Bar, with our mysterious brown bags and made two cappuccinos last for half-an-hour. It was a nice day, the sort of thing sisters in books do. It was expensive, though. Not the sort of thing you can do every Saturday. Still, I have to learn to be a bit less anxious about money.

After that we went and looked at an exhibition in an art gallery. Neither of us knows anything about art, but we're willing to learn, and anyway the exhibition was free. We didn't understand it. We didn't like it either. It was all half-finished looking pieces of sculpture, as if the sculptor had died in the middle of making a statue, and there were strange-looking things made out of chicken wire and dead light bulbs and what looked like lumps of plaster of paris. There was a television in a corner that kept playing the same thirty-second video of somebody running screaming through a tunnel, ending with their face looming right up at the camera and sort of exploding at you. Then they'd be running screaming through the tunnel again. The whole thing was green, like a black-and-white picture, only green, if you see what I mean. The last exhibition we saw there was patchwork quilts, all in lovely colours with feathery bits and sequins. It was much nicer.

The reason I mention this is that as we were leaving I caught sight of Mum. She was coming in the entrance door, as we were going out the exit. We were in a group of about six people all leaving together, so we would have been partially hidden by the bodies around us, and she was pushing the glass door with her right hand and looking back over her left shoulder to talk to somebody who was half beside her, half behind her, so that her raised arm shielded her face. I put my hand on Alva's arm to attract her attention and was about to say, There's Mum, look, what's she doing here, let's tell her it's terrible, not to waste her time, when I saw who it was Mum was talking to so animatedly. It was the proverbial tall dark stranger, though he wasn't especially hand-some, and too thin for his height. I noticed as he leaned across Mum to lend his weight also to the door that his hands were long and thin and rather white. I just stood for a moment and watched them, and then I half-turned and heaved against the heavy door and joined Alva, who by now was out on the footpath, putting up the hood of her anorak, as it was starting to drizzle.

I said: Let's run to the bus shelter, otherwise these paper bags will start to disintegrate. Biodegradable is all very well, but I don't want them biodegrading all over our lovely new skirts.

I never mentioned Mum, or the tall dark stranger.

Tuesday 20th May

Alva had extra hockey today. She's good, if only she would train a bit harder. Anyway, she's been picked for a team that has a match on Saturday, so she had no choice but to go to extra practice, and she wasn't able to come home with me, so we arranged that she'd go home with her friend Sarah afterwards, and Mum would pick her up from there later. That's how come Mum and I ended up doing the shopping together, without Alva, this evening. It was nice. I didn't have Alva nagging at me to buy chocolate biscuits, so I was able to concentrate on what I was doing much better. We went around together, pushing our trolley, and we discussed all our purchases rationally, tranquilly, in a grown-up way. It sounds a small thing, but those are the sort of situations that intimacy is built on, I feel.

They had boyscouts on the checkouts, doing the packing. They don't know much about packing shopping. They don't put the frozen things separately, so you can unload them quickly into the freezer, and they put mushrooms at the bottom of a bag, under big heavy things like tins of tomatoes and bunches of bananas, so you end up with mushroom paté by the time you get home. I was just thinking that if I had a little brother, I'd make sure he knew about putting the fragile things at the top. Then I remembered. It hadn't really struck me before that Gavin *is* our little brother. We always just think of him as belonging to Dad and Naomi. It's not the same as a real little brother, of course. We can't teach him things like putting the frozen foods together, but still, he is a little brother, it *is* a blood relationship.

I was thinking all this as I rescued a bag of hot-cross buns from under the toilet-duck, and I must have stopped in the middle of it, because I suddenly realised I was standing at the checkout with a bag of buns in one hand and a toilet-duck in the other, with a puzzled-looking little boyscout staring at me curiously. I met his eyes, like two little buttons in his freckly face, and I gave him a quick smile and said: Just rescuing the buns. We don't want them forest pine flavoured, do we?

Even as I said it I knew I was being silly and patronising, but I was trying to cover up because I was suddenly filled with guilt for thinking of Gavin as my little brother. It seemed a disloyal thought, disloyal to Mum, I mean.

I looked at her then, screwing up her eyes to read the total on the checkout machine – she was forty last year, and it's time she got glasses, I think – and I felt so sorry for her. She's just got her hair done. It's naturally thick and wavy, and it's a lovely honey colour. She wears it in a bouncy style, shaved up close at the back and then springing out from her head, but just as I looked at her peering anxiously to see how much this week, I saw that her face had got old and worried looking, and her lovely haircut looked as if it belonged to somebody else, somebody younger. But then she turned towards me and gave me her sunny smile and she looked OK again, and I felt relieved. I wanted to give her a hug and tell her it was all all right. But she would have been a bit surprised if I did that, so I just smiled back. Then I threw my eyes up and mouthed, Boyscouts! and grimaced. She nodded, but she threw twenty pence into their collection bucket just the same.

Wednesday 21st May

It happened again this evening. Mum was on the phone during my practising time. This time the other person rang her, though, so it's not her fault. I'm dying to know if it's the tall dark stranger. I hope so. Wouldn't it be great if Mum had a – I don't know how to put this – 'boyfriend' sounds too girlish, 'man' sounds too racy, 'partner' sounds too proprietorial, 'friend' sounds too coy. But maybe it was just somebody she got talking to outside the gallery. Maybe she was just telling him where the cloakroom was. Maybe they were just two people exchanging remarks on the street. But in that case, who is ringing her up? I just hope he's not married, that's all. Mum wouldn't dream of it if he is of course. I mean, I hope he's not married and pretending not to be.

Well! A great leap forward! Mum's going out tonight with Richard. Richard is her new gentleman caller. That's what she called him when she told us about him. It's a little joke, that, a reference to a play, I think. I don't know much about plays. Maths and science are really more my line than English.

She told us this morning at breakfast. I don't think she chose breakfast on purpose because it's a rushed meal and we have to leave first to catch the bus. I think she must have been working up to it for some time. She started to say something several times. Last week on the way home from the shopping I felt sure she was going to say something, but she doesn't talk much when she is driving. She has to concentrate on what she is doing.

I was a little bit disappointed that she told us both together, I have to say. I thought she might have spoken to me privately first, and then I would be able to say I knew all along and make a cryptic remark about the art exhibition. I was looking forward to that. It was going to be our little joke, but I could see she was struggling to find the words – which explains why she made the feeble joke about the gentleman caller – so I didn't say anything to make it more difficult for her. Alva went white and then burst into tears. Tears at breakfast are a bad start to any day.

I wanted to congratulate Mum, but I couldn't with Alva making a fuss. She wants to keep our mother to herself for ever and ever, to make a sort of shrine to a dead marriage of her. It's time she faced up to the fact that Dad is not coming back. Just because he remembers our birthdays and pays our school fees doesn't mean he wants to go back to being a proper father. He got a divorce six months ago. I don't know how he managed it. You still can't get a divorce here, even though we've had the referendum and everything. The laws haven't been fixed up yet. But Dad managed it. I think he got it in London. I thought Mum mightn't like that. She doesn't really approve of divorce, for religious reasons. But when it came to it, I think she was relieved that the whole thing was over.

Anyway, Mum's only known this man a few weeks, I'm sure of that. It's not as though she said she was going to marry him. Alva's like an over-protective parent who thinks that as soon as their child meets somebody they're going to get married! Still, it's hard on her. She desperately wants Dad back, even still, so I tried not to be too gruff with her. It's probably just as well it was breakfast time after all, and we had a bus to catch.

Friday 30th May

We finally got a chance to have a private chat, me and Mum. Alva went to Sarah's after school today again, and I came home on my own. Mum was home already when I got in. I love coming home on Fridays. I turned the key in the lock with a satisfying click and I swung my schoolbag through the front door. It landed with a thud at the foot of the stairs. Mum called out from the kitchen: Pick it up. Don't leave it there for someone to fall over.

Pick it up, I replied, imitating her voice loudly, pretending to be funny, though really I was a bit irritated. Don't leave it there for someone to fall over.

I could hear Mum's laugh as I picked up the offending schoolbag and slung it under the stairs where it lives. That made me feel better, hearing her laughing, I mean.

Alva is not careful with things. The whole house is strewn with her stuff. Mum and I are worn out picking up after her.

I bet you thought that was Alva, I said, as I came into the kitchen and plonked a kiss on Mum's face. I'm taller than her now and I have to bend down to kiss her. I don't like that. Parents are supposed to be bigger than their children. It makes me feel I have to be the grown-up around here.

Of course I didn't. I'd know your step anywhere, she said, handing me a cup of tea. I'd know even the way you turn the key in the lock.

Tell me more about Richard, I asked, fishing a tea-leaf out of my tea. Mum always makes tea with loose tea at the weekends. She says it's nicer, but we use teabags during the week, because they are more convenient. I love that first cup of real tea on a Friday afternoon. Not that I can really tell the difference in the taste, but it's like a little celebration of Friday.

I mean, I added slyly, I already know that he's tall and dark and thin.

Mum looked startled. I said nothing for a few minutes, just gave a knowing grin. Then I explained about seeing them going into the art gallery that Saturday. Mum plonked down on the chair opposite me and said: You can't do a *thing* in this city, not a single thing. It's nothing but an overgrown village.

In spite of what she was saying, you could hear in her voice that she was absolutely delighted. She was dying to know what I thought. I said I'd only caught a glimpse of him really. But she kept pressing me: didn't I think he dressed well, didn't he look distinguished? She was like a girl. I could have been talking to one of my friends from school: isn't he gorgeous, isn't he cool, don't you like the gear he wears? It was a bit of a shock, but I suppose love makes people like that. I probably used to say that sort of thing about Bob when I first started to go out with him. I suppose it is natural to want the people close to you to approve of the person you have chosen, or are considering choosing, as a partner. I wanted to join in with her and say yes, yes, enthusiastically, he's lovely, it's great.

And I do think it's great, it's exactly what I have been wanting for her all along, but somehow, when she turned shining eyes on me I just couldn't be as enthusiastic as she wanted me to be. I don't know why. And I suddenly couldn't understand why I had been so keen up to now for her to find a man. Why on earth should I have thought that that was what she needed in her life? It's all very confusing.

What's his family situation? I asked, lightly, looking out of the window. I felt like an old-fashioned father asking his daughter if her suitor's intentions were honourable. It was a peculiar situation to be in, everything the wrong way round. Maybe that's what made it so confusing.

Widower, she said.

Are you sure? I asked, watching intently, as next-door's cat stalked along the garden wall, and feeling even more like a protective parent.

Of course! she said. I was at his wife's funeral.

What? You could have knocked me over with the proverbial feather. This wasn't exactly the sort of proof of his marital status I'd had in mind. Surely they couldn't...

Not as a friend of his, Mum said hurriedly. I didn't even know him then. His daughter is a pupil. Several of the staff went. I didn't know her then either, except to see. But I thought the guidance counsellor should go.

Oh! I said, relieved. Still, I was a bit shaken. For a horrible moment I thought that Mum and this man had been, well, seeing each other while his wife was still alive. I didn't ask any more. So much for the jokey little chat we were going to have.

Is it OK if I go bowling with Bob tonight? I asked, partly because I needed to check, but partly because I wanted to change the subject, and partly also because I wanted to re-establish the roles. After all, she is the one in authority. It's up to her to approve of my boyfriend. Not the other way around.

Of course, Mum said, completely uninterested. I suppose I should be pleased that Bob is accepted as if he were part of the family. But somehow it made me feel hard done by, the way she just said, Of course, like that, without giving it another thought.

I don't know what to do about Alva, Mum said then, steering the conversation back. I said Alva would be all right. It was just her age. I remember fourteen. It's hard. But I didn't want to talk about Alva. I didn't want to talk at all any more. It's funny, I had imagined this conversation, looked forward to it, but now that it had happened, I felt sort of disappointed, empty.

Sunday 1st June

I can hardly believe I did this. It's not the sort of thing I do, normally. I never act on impulse. I don't even know why I did it, really. I was in such a funny mood last night. But now that it's happened, and I've slept on it and thought it over, I don't think I want to undo it.

I hadn't thought about it before, but suddenly it became clear to me last night that I never really liked bowling. It's the sort of thing people do when they are going out together. They go bowling, so we did it too. But there I was in the bowling alley, with those bright, bright lights, and all that echoey noise, people shouting and laughing in a hollow space and the incessant, irregular sound of bowling balls trundling along and banging in their channels and those gate things crashing down, and that smell of feet you get because people change their shoes, and I thought, This is a really horrible place, what am I doing here? Why am I not at home listening to Montserrat Caballé or watching a documentary about the economy of Rwanda or making popcorn with Alva or doing anything, really, rather than being here?

I suggested to Bob we should leave, and he said: But we've just got here. We've paid.

That struck home. You couldn't just walk out of something you'd paid for, so I stuck it out.

I won every game. The people we were with, mostly sixth-years, friends of Bob's, began to get a bit miffed that I was doing so well. They set out to try and beat me, but I just played better and better, I sent those pins flying left, right and centre.

Hey, you're really on top form tonight, Ashling, Bob said proudly, hanging his arm around my neck.

I could smell the mixture of fresh sweat and deodorant from his armpit, as he tightened his elbow, drawing my head in towards his body, and suddenly I started to gasp for air and pulled sharply away from him.

Now can we go? I asked. I think we've got our money's worth.

Poor Bob. He really looked put out. He'd paid for me as well as himself, not because he thinks the boy should pay, but because he knows money is much more of an issue in our family than it is in his. His father is director of some company or other. His mother too. They make burglar alarms, I think. Dreadful, anti-social things. It's not his fault. He's a nice person, he's kind and fair and thoughtful.

We walked home from the bowling alley. That was my idea. I

still had this feeling that I needed air, and I didn't want to pile into a bus, so we walked, even though it's a good two or three miles. We talked, all the way. We didn't argue. We just talked amicably, about the people who'd been at the alley with us. It was fun. I enjoyed it much more than the bowling, and I thought I had got over the feeling of claustrophobia I had got there. We laughed about how annoyed some of the others had got because I'd been winning.

But when we got to our house, I just didn't want to ask Bob in. Mum's usually up when I get in, and we sometimes make tea or cocoa before he goes home. But I didn't ask him in, and just as he leaned over to kiss me good night, I ducked under his arm and said: Bob, I don't really want to see you any more, at least not for the moment.

I don't know where I got the words from. If I had planned to say that, I'd never have worked up the courage. But they just came out by themselves. I was nearly as shocked as he was, listening to myself saying those words. But once they were out, I found myself liking the sound of them.

I'm sorry, I went on, and I genuinely was sorry. I like Bob. He's a good guy. I don't really understand why I felt like that, not wanting to see him. I didn't wait for him to answer. I just kissed him swiftly on the mouth and patted his arm consolingly. Then I flew in the gate, unlocked the door and shut it quickly behind me.

The hall light was on, but the rest of the house was in darkness. No Mum sitting up watching late-night movies and nodding off on the sofa. Oh well, I thought, maybe I don't really want to talk to her anyway. Maybe it's better that she's gone to bed. I considered making cocoa just for myself, but the thought of drinking it all by myself in the kitchen, with only the World Service for company, made me feel all lonely and sorry for myself, so I just switched off the hall light and slid up the stairs to bed. I felt sort of vacant, but at the same time my head was buzzing and it took ages to get to sleep. When I did sleep, I kept dreaming about bowling balls rumbling and banging along and the clashing sounds of the bowling alley.

Friday 6th June

I sent Bob a good luck card today. He's starting his exams on Monday. I didn't know whether to put *Love, Ashling*, or *Ashling XXX* or what. It seemed a bit dishonest to put love and kisses, when I've just broken up with him. In the end I just put *Ashling* and one X, but I scrawled it so you could interpret it as just a squiggle if you wanted to.

I didn't see him at school this week, because the exam classes were all out, working at home, revising for their exams. The rest of us had the tail end of our summer house exams early in the week, and then the last few days were really just clearing out. We helped to set up the exam halls, moving desks and so on. Team-work and co-operation are part of our school's philosophy, so we all mucked in. It was nice to be doing something different. Even fifth year can be a bit intense at times, so it is nice to get a bit of a break from academic work.

We have been advised to do a bit of school work over the summer, maybe re-reading history and reading ahead for English, that sort of thing, but to make sure we get a good break too, so we come back refreshed for the marathon year ahead – we're doing the Leaving next year. We were all told to go away for a bit, to get a really good break. Most people in our school come from well-off families. Lots of them are going to the Dordogne or Provence for

29

weeks on end, taking a house for the summer. Some of them even have their own holiday houses in these places. We'll be lucky if we get a week in a caravan at Brittas Bay. I'd love to go somewhere nice. Even a package holiday would be good, but it's out of our range. The summer is our leanest time financially, because of Mum not working.

Bob and I had a loose arrangement to go camping and youth-hostelling this summer with a gang of friends, just to Glenmalure or somewhere like that. Oh well.

Saturday 7th June

Spent the day walking around the local shops, restaurants and cafés, looking for a summer job. I think I've left it too late. Everywhere already has people for the summer.

Sunday 8th June

Mum went to a concert last night with Richard. She says he knows next to nothing about music, so she's going to teach him. Alva went to an end-of-term school disco. I thought I was going to be the only one with nowhere to go, but Mrs Merrigan – Joan, I must remember to call her Joan – who lives across the road asked me to babysit, so at least I didn't have to sit at home and watch *Kenny Live* by myself. I watched it in Merrigans' instead. At least, *Kenny Live* is off for the summer, I discovered, so I watched some game show on UTV, with young Darren Merrigan jumping all over the furniture brandishing an amazingly realistic looking machine gun and making appalling trutt-utt-utt-utt-utt noises and Tanya Merrigan sobbing quietly in a corner in her dressing gown. I don't think I've ever seen that girl not sobbing, except when she is asleep. She's like a little one-woman tear-factory. I felt a bit like joining her last night, but I thought that wouldn't really be in the spirit of the contract. They're never sent to bed before the babysitter comes. Their mother says she likes to present being babysat as a treat, so they don't make too much fuss about her going out. She doesn't call me the babysitter, she calls me the visitor, and she gives me two Kinder Surprise eggs when I arrive that I am supposed to give them as a present.

They make a fuss about her going out anyway, which just shows that bribery doesn't work. She could save herself the price of the Kinder Surprises, but it's probably guilt money. Not that I think she should feel guilty about going out once in a while, even if she does always seem to go out with creeps. Alva's theory is that once a creep meets the children, he backs off like mad, and Joan has to wait for another creep to come along.

Bring Bob, Joan said brightly when she rang. I didn't answer her about that part, and when I turned up on my own she didn't ask where he was, or if he was coming later. It's amazing really how nobody has noticed the Bob-shaped gap yet.

I hope Richard isn't a creep. I mean, I hope he wouldn't back off if he met us. If he did, I suppose that would mean he wasn't worth the candle anyway, but still, it would be dreadful for Mum. I'd better talk to Alva about this. We don't want her frightening him off. She's quite liable to. On second thoughts, maybe that would only give her ideas. She might set out to put him off. No, I don't think I'll say anything, just try to keep her well out of his way.

Sunday 15th June

We are quite conservative about Sundays in our house. We always spend them together, just the three of us, except those very occasional weekends when Alva and I go to visit Dad and Naomi and Gavin. So it was a bit of a shock when Mum announced after lunch today that she was going out for a little while. It's not so bad to have a summer Sunday spoilt, because we're together a lot anyway in the summer, but even so.

With Richard? asked Alva, resentfully.

Mum is defensive about Richard when she is talking to Alva. She knows Alva doesn't like it that she has a boyfriend. She never stops talking to me about him, every opportunity she gets she mentions his name. I'm starting to get tired of hearing about him, but she keeps quiet about him when Alva is there. She still hasn't noticed that Bob isn't around any more. Neither has Alva.

Yes, with Richard, Mum said, in a dignified tone.

She's always with him, Alva hissed, as Mum left the room. She has no time for us any more. She prefers him to us.

That is ridiculous, Alva, I said, and I know it is ridiculous, she couldn't possibly prefer him to us, I know that. But still, a bit of me feels she shouldn't go out with him on a Sunday, that it's not fair to us. Sometimes it's hard to see things from the other person's point of view, even if it's your mother.

Mum put her head around the sitting room door when she'd got her jacket on, to say goodbye. We were listening to a Bach organ concerto and playing chinese chequers. I love Bach. Alva loves chinese chequers. Mum sang out, I won't be long, her words floating across the room to us over the music. Neither of us replied, which was a bit mean of us, but I suppose we were both feeling hurt.

Let's go and get ourselves a Magnum each, I suggested to Alva, after Mum had left.

Magnums are wickedly expensive, but they're delicious. Bob

loves them. It's funny how many things remind me of Bob.

Yeh, let's, said Alva. Let's live dangerously.

It's so easy to distract her. It's hard to believe this same Alva wanted to go to a rave only a month ago. I don't think she has a clue what a rave is.

Wednesday 18th June

I've landed myself a holiday job. I just happened to be in the local bookshop, trying to decide if I could afford to buy *A Brief History of Time*. I've ordered it from the library, but I won't get it from there till the end of August, and by then I'll be nearly back to school. It's the sort of thing you need to take a summer to read, I think. I had decided that the best thing was probably to try the ILAC library, so I was putting the paperback copy back on the shelf when I noticed a little hand-printed notice on a cork notice-board beside the bookcase. It was so self-effacing, it almost looked as if it didn't want to be read. It said:

> *Wanted:*
> *Temporary staff*
> *Must be literate*
> *Apply to Mr George*

George must be a surname. I thought at first it was like one of those old family firms, where you call the junior members of the family 'Mr' followed by their christian name.

I didn't stop to think. That only makes me nervous. I went straight up to the desk and asked to speak to Mr George, and I was shown into a poky little office at the back, piled high with books and papers. There were coffee rings on the few places on the desk where you could see the surface, and there was an old-fashioned manual typewriter, the kind with a red and a blue ribbon, and the place smelt of paraffin, from an old heater he had snuffling away in a corner. The air was like cotton wool. He didn't exactly interview me. He didn't ask my age, or where I was at school, but he asked if I was literate. I said I was, but I wasn't literary.

Hmph, he said (he was very large and old, just the type to say Hmph), well, if you're literate enough to tell the difference, that'll do. It's £2.50 an hour, start Monday, half-past eight till six, late night Thursday till eight-thirty, every other Saturday off. Until end of July. Lad comes back then. Right?

He had an English accent, like on *Emmerdale*. I don't know what he's doing in our local bookshop, but he seems to be the boss. I'm looking forward to starting on Monday. I have no idea if £2.50 an hour is a decent rate. It sounds OK. It's more than I get for babysitting anyway.

Tuesday 24th June

Working in a bookshop is exhausting. My feet are killing me. All that standing. But it's only for a few weeks. You can stick anything for a few weeks. I like going into the store-room at the back, next door to Mr George's office. It's completely airless and muffled in there, but there is this intense smell of paper that I love. My fingers are starting to develop an extra layer of skin already, from handling the books. They get surprisingly dusty.

Wednesday 25th June

Bob came into the bookshop today. It's more than three weeks, but I have managed to avoid him, until now, because it's the summer holidays. It would have been tricky in term time. He was clearly surprised to see me, standing there at the till, but he acted really cool. Still, I had the advantage over him: I saw him first. I had time to duck down behind the counter and cool my burning face with my hands and let my heart stop racing. It wasn't excitement or even embarrassment. It was just shock, I think.

Hiya, Ashling, he said, handing me a copy of *Sense and Sensibility* and a fiver. It's terrible how cheap these classics are.

He didn't even avert his eyes or shuffle from foot to foot or anything. I felt like doing those things, but since he didn't, I decided to brave it out too.

Oh, hi Bob, I said, trying to sound ultra-cool. How're the exams going?

I suddenly felt terribly guilty. Was it very mean of me to break up with him just before the most important exam of his life? Yes, it was, selfish and thoughtless. I may have ruined this boy's career prospects.

Fine, fine, he said. Thanks for the card, by the way. Only German left. Tomorrow. I saw the movie, he added, indicating the book. Last night. I went with an old friend of mine.

What was he doing going to the cinema in the middle of his exams? *I* want to see that film, but I have been putting it off because there is nobody to go with. Not since there's been no Bob in my life. I got a sudden stab of nostalgia. I realised then that I didn't feel dismayed that he was going to the cinema in the middle of his exams. I felt dismayed that he was going with somebody who wasn't me. But maybe that was what I was meant to feel. Maybe that was why he was telling me.

Good, was it? I asked coldly.

Brill, he said, absolutely bloody brill.

He never used words like that when he was with me. Brill, I mean, not bloody.

Oh? I said, trying to sound as if I didn't really care, trying to sound half-distracted, as if I were only making small talk. I thrust the book at him, sellotaped into its paper bag.

She just finished her Junior Cert last week, he offered then. She needed a break.

Who? I asked, but my mouth was dry.

Becky, he said.

Who's Becky? I asked.

Oh, just someone I know from way back when, he said. She used to live near me. We went to playschool together. She's years younger, but she was sent at two, because her mother couldn't cope with her at home, and I was still there, because my mother couldn't cope with the idea of sending me to real school. He gave a snorting sound, which I think was meant to be a laugh. I didn't laugh with him. I used to mind her, he went on, because I was the oldest and she was the youngest.

Meaning they were 'just good friends', I suppose.

Oh? How did she get on? I asked. Your playschool friend, I mean.

Fine, Bob said. But she's not at playschool any more.

Well, that was pretty obvious.

She recommended I should buy this (at this point he waved the paper bag containing the book in the air), since I enjoyed the film so much.

I never recommended books to him. I don't know much about books, really, though I know a bit more since I've been working in the bookshop. Last week, I was able to tell a customer who said she wanted *Surely* by Jane Eyre that what she was really looking for was a copy of *Shirley* by Charlotte Brontë. I don't think she's going to enjoy it, but I sold it to her anyway, which is what I'm here for.

I had tried to get him interested in music, Bob, I mean. I took him to concerts. I even made him come to some of our rehearsals – I'm in an orchestra at school, you have to be with the double-bass, it's not exactly a solo instrument – trying to get him to share some of the excitement of it all. But all he ever said was, very nice, very nice. He never said it was bloody brill, that's for sure.

Thursday 26th June

Mum told us today she'd been asked to lunch at Richard's on Sunday. We didn't say anything. Alva didn't because she is completely obnoxious on the subject of Richard. I didn't because I was taken aback at the idea that she would go out to Sunday lunch. It's one thing going out on a Sunday afternoon, but Sunday lunch is sacrosanct.

She let it hang in the air for a moment. Then she added, He asked me to bring you two as well. He'd like to meet you. And he'd like you to meet his daughter too.

Oh god! his daughter, I thought. I'd sort of forgotten about the daughter. I didn't really want to meet her. Girls of that age are so tedious. I prefer small children, boys of my own age, and adults. I bet she's another Alva. But it was obvious we were going to have to meet Richard, and if he and Mum felt the relationship had got to the point where we had to meet the daughter as well, then we just had to, that was all there was to it.

Alva was eating ice-cream, and she just went on spooning it in, unconcernedly, as if Mum had said it was her turn to wash up. I tried to catch her eye, but she was staring at the wall.

That's nice of him, Mum, I said brightly. Isn't it Alva?

Alva still went on eating her ice-cream like an automaton.

Alva, I said loudly, pressing down hard on her toe under the table.

Ow! she said. That hurts, Ashling. I got a belt of a hockey stick on that toe.

I'm sorry, Alva, I said, I didn't realise. But we'll look forward to that, won't we? Lunch with Mum's friend Richard. Won't we?

I pressed again on her toe.

Yeh, ow, stop, yeh, yeh, we will, great, yeh, ow!

I mentioned then that I had sold Bob a book yesterday, to change the subject. Also, I thought it would be a good idea to mention his name. They might think it odd if I never did.

Nobody must have thought much of this as a conversational opening, because nobody said anything. Is it me? Or is it Bob? How come nobody notices what I'm doing with my life?

Sunday 29th June

I told Alva I didn't think she should wear her jeans to Richard's house. Not the ones with the tears in them anyway. She sulked at that, but she said she would look and see what she could find. I thought she would probably wear one of her long dresses. That's all she ever wears, disreputable jeans and long dresses, as if she is afraid someone might catch a glimpse of her legs. They must be pale and atrophied, like those white worms that live under stones and never see the sun. But she appeared in a neat little polo neck and the navy tartan skirt she bought that day when we went into town to spend her birthday money. It looked really nice on her. She has a good figure, only you don't often get to see it. She even had navy tights to match. I bet she nicked those from my room.

She'd never have a pair of navy tights of her own. She's always nicking my stuff.

I laughed when I saw her in the tartan skirt, because I was wearing the skirt I'd bought that day, too. I often wear mine, because I like it. I don't think Alva has worn hers at all since she bought it, except once, just to give it an outing. She says wearing a skirt reminds her too much of school uniforms.

Will this do? she asked. Oh, and I borrowed these, she added, opening her hand.

Lying in her pink little palm were four identical pearl stud ear-rings. I must explain that Mum is fanatical about pearl ear-rings. She must have about ten pairs. I think the only reason she let us get our ears pierced was that she fondly imagined us in pearl studs. But Alva goes around all the time with enamel fried eggs dangling from her ears, and I usually wear dream-catchers, except at school, of course, where we wear silver sleepers.

What are you doing with those, Alva? I asked. Did you take them from Mum's room? You're terrible. You know she hates you taking her stuff, because she has to go all over the house looking for it.

She'll like this, though, Alva said with a grin. Here, you take two.

So we both put the ear-rings in. They made us look about twenty.

Now we're respectable enough for the great Richard, aren't we? said Alva, grinning into my bedroom mirror.

She had obviously decided to get into the spirit of the thing, instead of trying to kick against it. I think that's pretty big of her, actually, because I know she finds it hard. I put my arm across her shoulders and gave her a little squeeze, our eyes smiling at each other in the mirror, to show I appreciated it.

Just as well the Boyzone crew can't see you now, I said. They'd never recognise you.

Mum blinked when she saw us. Then she noticed the ear-rings and she laughed. Tweedle-dum and Tweedle-dee, she said. But you could see she was nervous. I was glad we'd made a bit of an effort, for her sake.

Which is more than can be said for Richard's daughter. It turns out her name is Cindy. It's all right for a doll or a supermodel, but a real girl called Cindy! She certainly didn't look like a super-model. She wore a T-shirt that looked as if she'd slept in it and awful jeans. Not only had they tears in them, I think they were actually dirty.

Their house is really lovely. It's big and old and it has a bay window and a marble fireplace and real glass chandeliers and a beautiful walnut piano. I was itching to try it out, but it looked as if nobody ever played it. They have a parquet floor in the dining room and a persian rug. At least, I don't know if it's persian, but it's beautiful, all lovely rich reds and blues. Everything looked as if it came out of an antique shop. Even the pouffe in the sitting room was real leather. And the food was delicious too, proper Sunday food. Lamb I think we had. Richard cooked it himself. He is quite proud of his cooking. You'd expect somebody interested in food to be fatter.

He fussed around with chafing dishes and chargers – I never even heard of these things until I heard him talking about them – at a great rate, but Cindy just sat there and looked bored. She hardly said a word all through the meal. I thought at first maybe she was shy, and I tried to say a few things to her, but she didn't pick up any of my conversational openings, so Alva and I ended up just saying things like pass the butter. We were trying very hard, for Mum's sake.

Her dad produced a bottle of red wine. He's really a very nice man, or seems to be. He offered me some. I had a little drop, but I don't really drink, so I topped it up with water. I think that was a mistake, because it tasted terrible. Alva got Coke, and I was sorry I hadn't asked for some too. But Cindy really lashed into the wine, and after her third glass she was jabbering away about nothing in particular, mostly stories about friends of hers, particularly somebody called Lisa, which were of no interest to us. I think Mum quite enjoyed some of it, because she knew the people she was talking about, from school. She talked about the teachers a bit as well, and told Mum what their nicknames were. They weren't very original. And she was rude about the food. Alva said the dessert was scrumptious, and she looked witheringly at her and said it was scum, not scrum.

Then she passed out. I felt sorry for Richard, trying to make it all seem normal. We had to pretend not to notice. It was so embarrassing. Then Mum had a brainwave.

Let's all go for a walk. Palmerston Park, maybe? (They live quite near there.) Or what about Dún Laoghaire pier?

That's a great idea, said Richard. A nice brisk walk on Dún Laoghaire pier – just the thing to sobe... eh, blow away the cobwebs. Come on, Cindy, wake up, there's a good girl.

He had to put her jacket on her. She was too drunk to do it for herself. He managed to get her into the back of his car, and we all drove off to the sea. We put Cindy between us, Alva and me, and sort of propelled her along the pier like that. She came to after a bit.

It wasn't my idea of a great way to spend a Sunday afternoon, but you could see that Mum was enjoying it, in spite of everything. You could tell just by the way she looked at Richard that she's really fallen for him. I hope it all turns out all right for her. I don't want her getting hurt. Not again.

Tuesday 1st July

Alva threw a wobbly yesterday. A real wobbly. I haven't seen her like that since she was a small child, not even when Dad left. Then she just cried and cried. But this was anger. She stamped her foot and said all the usual things. It's not fair was the main one. That really wasn't a very good argument. I don't see how fair comes into it.

This was all because Mum said she was going away for the weekend with Richard. We're going to Dad this weekend. That was arranged ages ago. So it's no skin off our nose what Mum does. She didn't even need to tell us. She could just have gone off on the quiet and been back before us and we'd never have known. What's really not fair is that Alva is giving her hell when all she's doing is trying to be honest and up-front with us, telling us she is going away with him.

I tried to reason with her, Alva, I mean. I said Mum needed to form new relationships, and that it wasn't fair of us to try to stop her.

She doesn't *need* new relationships, Alva kept insisting, she's got us. We're relations, the closest she's got.

The word I wanted to use to Alva was 'childish', but I knew if I said that was how she was behaving it would only make her worse. And I must admit that a little bit of me is on her side. I was a bit shocked at the idea of Mum going away for the weekend with this man she hardly knows. I have to remind myself that *she* probably knows him quite well. It's just that *we* don't know him so well. And he seems such a nice man. Maybe it would have been better if Mum hadn't said anything to Alva about it. But the cat is out of the bag now. Mum is too honest for her own good.

I brought Alva to work with me today, to keep her out of Mum's way. I introduced her to Mr George – I found out by the way that George really is his christian name, his surname is Chiswick, isn't it a hoot that he calls himself Mr George? – and said I was minding her for the day. He said he wasn't running a creche. He can be a bit surly at times. I said of course not, but that she would earn her keep. I put her dusting books in the storeroom. I could hear her sneezing from my spot at the till. Then I sent her out to the bakery for doughnuts for everyone at 11 o'clock and I got her to make the tea. We usually all just snatch a cup of tea when we can, so it was a treat to have somebody serve it up. Mr George complained that the doughnuts were too sugary and that we would get sticky fingerprints all over the books, but he was stuffing his doughnut into his mouth as he said this, so I wasn't too concerned.

I paid for the doughnuts myself. And I slipped out at lunchtime and bought Alva some sheet music, Carolan's concerto, transposed for the flute. She said she wanted to learn some traditional music, for a change. It's lovely to have money to be able to do things like that. It certainly smoothes things over. Maybe I'll be a negotiator when I grow up. I'd be good at it, as long as they give me a doughnut budget. Bob always said that a doughnut mightn't solve a problem, but it made you feel better while you were thinking about it. Bob was dead on in a lot of ways. I have to admit that I miss him.

I think the less said about the weekend the better. Things were very tense in Dad's house. He and Naomi were barely civil to each other. I kept feeling that if we weren't there they'd have been at each other's throats. It's horrible to feel like a visitor in your own father's house. But then, I have to remember it is Naomi's house too, and as far as she is concerned we *are* visitors.

I should point out that Mum and Dad separated amicably. Fairly. I mean, it wasn't as though there was violence or anything. I think there might have been a bit of a drink problem with Dad, I have to say. But he never got aggressive when we was drunk. He just got slobbery and sentimental.

There was Naomi, of course. She's Dad's 'partner' now. She probably calls herself his 'fiancée', now that he's got a divorce. It always amuses me how people use that word to be respectable. But back then she was 'the other woman'. I like her. She's a good laugh. She's much younger than Dad, closer to us in age, really, and she talks to me about hairstyles and fashions and makeup. I never have those conversations with my friends. I think maybe girls today are more serious than they were even ten years ago.

But I haven't forgotten that this is the woman that Dad left Mum for, and no matter how civilised Mum is about it, she did go through hell at the time, and basically it was Naomi's fault, or rather Dad's and Naomi's together. I think it is noble of Mum to let us come here for weekends. But that's Mum all over. She is so fair and balanced. That's why I feel so strongly that she deserves a new relationship of her own. But try telling Alva that!

I asked Mum if she had enjoyed her weekend. She said she had a whale of a time. It was great to hear her saying that. They had super food and delicious wine and a jacuzzi. I've never been in a jacuzzi. It sounds sort of weird, but nice. She got back late last night. It was a pity they couldn't have had an extra day. Mum's free all the time at the moment, apart from her commitments to the garden, which she takes nearly as seriously as other people take their jobs, but Richard has to be at his desk by eight o'clock every morning. I think he works in computers. People in jobs like that seem to kill themselves. I thought computers were supposed to make life easier, not harder, but it doesn't seem to work like that.

Wednesday 9th July

Mr George asked me if Alva would like to work in the bookshop, just covering at lunchtimes, for a few weeks. She's thrilled. She's never had a job before. She's starting tomorrow.

Thursday 10th July

Mum is gone into one of her distracted moods again, as if she is worried about something, but when I ask her if everything is all right, she just mutters yes, yes, and moves away. I hope everything is all right between her and Richard. I think it is, because he still rings often, and when he does she's all of a flutter. I think that's very sweet, at her age.

Alva is doing fine at the job. The other people in the shop all treat her as a pet, rather than a colleague. This is not very good for her character. It means she gets away with not doing very much work. She just swans around being charming, and they fall for it. People always do with Alva. I don't understand it.

Bob came into the shop again yesterday. I was in the storeroom getting some more copies of *Sophie's World* for the dumpbin at the front, and when I came out with my arms full of books, there he was, sort of lingering near the cashdesk. It's quite dark in the storeroom, and when you come out of there, the people in the shop are like shadow-puppets moving against the light from the street, until your eyes adjust again to the daylight, so I just saw this Bob-shape sort of hovering in front of me, all fuzzy and purply-coloured around the edges, like a vision. My heart did a little flip and moved up a gear, and I could feel my whole circulation system racing around my body as if it was in a terrible hurry. I wasn't sure it was he, because of the shadowy effect, but then he spoke, and my heart did another little flip, and went into an even higher gear. I could feel the books starting to slip, and I had to make a conscious effort to hold on to them. I didn't want them cascading all over the floor and getting damaged.

I can't remember what it was that Bob actually said. It was more the sound of his voice that I remember. It's quite a gravelly voice, and you can feel it as much as hear it. I bet a deaf person would be able to sense it, the way they are supposed to be able to feel music. He must have come deliberately to see me, because I don't think he bought anything. He asked about Mum. Then, quite casually, he asked if I would meet him for a cup of coffee after work.

I put the books on the counter and started to line them up into groups of three. I didn't answer about the coffee. I didn't know what to say. I wanted to have a coffee with him. I wanted to sit down opposite him and have a good long chat, and I wanted him to play with my fingers as I spoke and push my hair back behind my ears the way he used to, and to walk me home with his arm around me and to wrap me up in a hug and give me some of those wonderful kisses of his, but I knew I would want him to turn around then and just go away and leave me alone. It wouldn't be fair to do that. To spend time with him, enjoy his company, take comfort from him and then wave him goodbye again.

I was just thinking all this through, when I heard that gravelly voice again, closer to my ear this time, repeating the invitation to coffee, and I said No, no, quite firmly, maybe it even sounded hysterical, because he just turned and walked out of the shop, without saying anything more, and I was left senselessly shuffling books and counting them one-two-three, one-two-three under my breath, for something to concentrate on until my heart slowed down again.

I've been trying to understand why I broke up with Bob. I like him, and I miss him, and, outside my immediate family, I don't think I know anyone as well as I know him. But I just don't want to be involved with him right now. It's nothing to do with him, really. I think it's all mixed up with the Mum-and-Richard business. Bob's just a complication I don't need in my life at the moment.

Monday 21st July

All hell broke loose here last night. Dad turned up on the doorstep at nearly midnight, with Gavin in his arms. I was asleep, so I didn't hear his car pulling up, but I faintly heard the doorbell, through my dream. Then there were these voices in the hall, and the sound of a child crying, and I gradually woke up. When I got downstairs, there was Mum in her dressing gown, with her hair in a hairnet –

I didn't know she possessed such a thing – standing at the door, talking in fierce whispers. I don't know why she was whispering when there was so much noise going on anyway, but I suppose it's a natural reaction when you know people are asleep. There was an icy draft in the hall. I was just in my pyjamas and slippers, and my teeth started to chatter. Mum swung around when she heard that and then she dragged whoever she was whispering at into the hall and closed the door. It was then I realised it was Daddy. Gavin's face was red and wet, and he had one fat fist in his mouth and the other hand was flailing about in anger or distress or something.

At first I thought there was something wrong with Gavin, that that's what all this was about. Mum and I got Dad and Gavin into the kitchen, which was nearly as cold as the hall, with that heavy, almost damp sort of cold you get in a north-facing room at night time, even in the summer. The fluorescent lights don't help to make it any more cheerful, but it was better than standing in the hall, expecting Alva to appear at any moment. Whatever was up, Alva would only have made things worse. She has this knack.

Dad put Gavin down on the kitchen table, as if he was a bag of shopping or a parcel, and I noticed that he was wearing his pyjamas under his dungarees. Dad sat down at the table and put his head in his hands, ignoring Gavin, who went on wailing loudly, through his slimy fist. It was so strange to see Dad sitting there. He hasn't been in this house for nearly four years, but he sat down automatically at his place at the table, beside the fridge. We always used to say he sat there so he could monitor everything everyone ate. Since he left, we sort of moved gradually around out of our old places – it's a round table – to fill in the gap, and now Dad's old place doesn't really exist any more. It's been partially taken over by me on one side and Mum on the other. He still managed to shift the chair into the old spot, though, obviously without thinking.

When I saw that Dad wasn't taking any notice of Gavin, I decided the problem couldn't be with the child, but he was crying so bitterly I still checked him over for bruises and scratches as I mopped his face with tissues. I took his fist out of his mouth and dried it. He went on bawling as I did this, his mouth hanging open and a stream of saliva hanging from it, like a thread dropped by a spider onto the bib of his dungarees. I wiped it up and dried his face and around his mouth, and then I gently pushed his chin up until his mouth closed. He looked surprised when I did that, and he went on snuffling, but he didn't open his mouth again, just sat there glumly on the tweed table mat that Dad hadn't noticed was under him, his eyes streaming and little sobs escaping now and then. His little tummy heaved when he sobbed.

I reached up to the top press and got him a Kit-Kat. I thought that would cheer him up. It didn't exactly elicit a smile, but his big round eyes seemed to get even rounder in his big round face. He showed intense interest in it and opened it very gingerly, breaking the fingers carefully apart and then commencing to eat them solemnly, one by one, with small precise bites. It was amazing, considering how carefully he applied himself to the task of eating the Kit-Kat, that he still managed to smear chocolate all over the lower half of his face and get chocolate crumbs down his front, onto the table top and lodged between his damp little fingers. There is really only a very thin coating of chocolate on a Kit-Kat, but a three-year-old can manage to distribute it very widely.

While all this was going on, Mum and Dad were deep in a

whispered, urgent conversation. I was trying very hard not to listen, as I felt it was not the sort of conversation that anyone should overhear. Dad smelt of drink. I don't think he was actually drunk, but he certainly shouldn't have been driving, especially not with the baby. It crossed my mind that Mum couldn't send him home like that.

I would have made some tea, only I was afraid Gavin might fall off the table if I left him, and I couldn't think of any place else to put him, apart from the floor, but I thought that was too cold. I started to croon nursery rhymes to him, not so much to soothe him as to make a noise so that I wouldn't have to hear the grownups talking. I was afraid of what I might hear.

Gavin liked it when I sang to him. He even smiled when he recognised a rhyme. He'd finished his Kit-Kat by now, and he started to clap and sing along with me, humming when he didn't know the words. After a while he lifted up his arms, to be picked up, so I gathered him up and we waltzed around the kitchen. Dad and Mum were still talking, so I opened the kitchen door and waltzed out into the hall. The hall smelt of carpet, something you don't notice during the day. By now Gavin's head had started to loll against my shoulder, and he had got heavier. His solid little body felt soft and tough at the same time.

I waltzed into the sitting room. It smelt of carpet in there too. Perhaps all carpeted rooms smell like that at night. I laid Gavin down on the sofa, and I tucked the old crocheted rug that we usually drape over the sofa, to hide the stains and the worn patches, over his sleeping little body. His mouth fell open, showing all his tiny little milk teeth. I pushed his chin up again gently to close it, and he tossed his head from side to side, his silky brown hair slithering across his forehead as he did so, and ground his teeth, but his mouth stayed closed. He breathed so quietly I had to put my ear close to his face to hear him. He made little gasping sounds as he breathed in, but he breathed out on a silent air flow. I stayed for a while, in the semi-darkness (I'd left the door ajar), listening to the shallow rhythm, and then I slipped away.

There was a crack of light still under the kitchen door, and I could hear their voices rising and falling. I went back to bed and lay there rigid, my feet like two blocks of ice and my eyes wide open. I knew I would be awake for hours and hours, but then suddenly it was morning and Mum was calling me for breakfast. I ran down the stairs, sure that Gavin would have fallen off the sofa and be lying in a snivelling heap on the sitting-room floor, but there was no Gavin there, just the multicoloured rug in a bundle at the end of the sofa.

Mum looked really drawn, as if she had lain awake most of the night. Goodness knows what time she got rid of Dad at. And how had she done that? She couldn't have let him drive. She must have driven them herself.

Don't ask, love, she said, as I sat down at the table. And don't, for heaven's sake, breathe a word of this to Alva.

As if I would! But I had a quick look out at the front, and sure enough, Mum's car was in the drive. I could have sworn it was in the garage last night.

Tuesday 22nd July

Mum didn't get up this morning. She's one of those people who can't lie in bed once they are awake, so it's very unlike her not to be singing in the kitchen at half-past seven. She usually calls me at about eight, but I'm often already awake, listening to her moving around downstairs, the fridge door squeaking open and shutting with a soft thud, Mum's pattery little footsteps on the vinyl, her sweet, rather breathy soprano voice lifted up over the clinking of the breakfast dishes, telling us that she dreamt she dwelt in marble halls, or calling out to sweet Caroline. (She has a funny combination of musical tastes.) It's one of my favourite times of the day, just lying there in the warm, knowing I have a few minutes still left in bed, listening to those comfortable sounds.

But not this morning. I woke at about a quarter past eight and leapt out of bed. The house was silent. Alva never gets up without physical encouragement. It was half past by the time I'd showered and dressed, and there was still no sound except the water filling back into the cylinder in the hot press on the landing. I thought I'd better check up on Mum, make sure she was OK. I had a moment of fear that maybe she'd slipped off somewhere in the night. A ridiculous idea, but it was like one of those leftover fears from childhood that still surface occasionally. And maybe not all that ridiculous. After all, she drove off the other night with Dad.

Her bedroom was in darkness. She has very thick curtains, so even in the summer it's dark in there when the curtains are closed. But I could hear her breathing, so I knew she was there. I knew she was awake too, because of the quality of her breathing, but she didn't say anything, as if she was pretending to be asleep.

Are you OK, Mum? I asked the small mound that I could make out, now that my eyes had become accustomed to the twilight, under the duvet.

She groaned.

Mum! I squeaked, panicking. Are you OK?

No, she muttered. Sick as a dog. Must be a tummy bug.

Would you like some tea? I asked.

Earl Grey, she answered. Black and weak. And could you bring a bucket or a basin or something?

She always asks for Earl Grey when she's ill. I made it quickly, in the cup, because I was rushing out for work, and flew upstairs with it and a large white bowl I found under the sink. I also brought a towel, a packet of tissues and a little bottle of eau de cologne, which I thought might be refreshing.

She was sitting up in bed this time. At least she wasn't too sick to plump up her pillows. She took the tea gratefully, and waved to me to put the other things down. She winced when I drew the curtains. She looked so pale in the morning light.

Take away the eau de cologne, please, she said, wrinkling up her nose in disgust. The smell makes me want to get sick.

It's not exactly Chanel No. 5, but I thought that was rather a strong reaction, considering the bottle wasn't even open. I popped it in the pocket of my jacket and said goodbye. I didn't have time for my own breakfast, but I didn't mention that.

When Alva appeared in the shop at lunchtime, I asked her how Mum was. She looked puzzled.

She's fine, she said. Not a bother. She was cleaning the oven when I left.

Wednesday 23rd July

Mum looked a bit peaky this morning at breakfast, but she said she was fine. She was quite rosy-cheeked by this evening, though, when I saw her next. Alva had gone to Pizzaland with her friends, blowing all her bookshop money in one go, no doubt. I made an omelet for Mum and me, with cheese and parsley. We often have one when Alva is out, because she doesn't like eggs.

Whew! Eau de cologne, Mum said, as I leant over to put her

half of the omelet on her plate, and she went quite white. In your pocket, Ashling. Take it out, throw it away!

I patted my pocket, and sure enough the little phial I'd put there yesterday morning was still there. I drew it out, and Mum made a face.

OK, I said, I didn't know you hated it that much. Here, I'll get rid of it altogether.

I tossed it into the bin.

Is everything all right between Dad and Naomi? I asked, now that I had Mum on her own in the house.

No, she said. Poor little Gavin.

She wasn't going to say any more, and I could see that she didn't want to be quizzed, so I just went on eating my omelet. I hope they're not splitting up or anything. Dad's crazy about Gavin. He couldn't bear it if Naomi left him and took Gavin with her. I presume she would, if she did.

Thursday 24th July

I found Mum crying in the hall when I came home from work today. She was sitting on the telephone seat, and she was stroking the telephone with both hands, as if it were alive, as if it were a puppy or a sick child. It must be Dad, I thought. Or Gavin. He must have kidnapped him.

Mum! I gasped, What is it, what's wrong? Is it Gavin?

Yes, she spluttered. Sort of.

What? What? Has Dad done something stupid?

Yes, she said again, dabbing at her eyes with a paper hanky. Sort of.

Oh Mum! I gasped, dropping to the floor at her feet. That's terrible. Did you ring the police, or what?

The police? The *police*? Ashling, what are you talking about? Why would I ring the police?

Because if Dad's run away with Gavin, he has to be stopped.

Run away? With Gavin?

And then, this is rather terrible, but she started to laugh. It was that sort of hysterical laughing that people do when they're just on the edge of crying, and it was horrible to listen to.

When you've quite finished, I said, coldly, because I was feeling very left out of the joke, maybe you'll explain to me what's going on.

Oh, my poor Ashling, Mum said, and she pulled my head onto her lap and started to stroke my hair. I'm sorry. I just mean that I can see how upsetting all this is for Alva, and Cindy as well, and just looking at little Gavin here the other night, bawling his head off because his parents had been rowing... Well, it all began to seem so muddled somehow, and I thought the best thing would be to stop seeing Richard. That's what I meant when I said it sort of has something to do with your dad and Gavin.

I pulled my head out of her lap and put my two hands up and caught her gently by the ears, the way I used to do when I was a small child. I rocked her head from side to side and knocked my forehead gently against hers. Oh, Mum, I said. It's not fair. Your happiness is at stake here. I felt a bit like a character in a soap opera, saying that, but I meant it.

Happiness, she said, as if it were a word she hadn't heard before. Happiness, she said again, as if she were turning it over in her mind, the way you might turn over a strange new fruit from some exotic land.

Yes, well, she said then, as if putting the fruit down again, I have to put you and Alva first.

Don't be silly, I protested. Alva will get over it. She's just being bolshy. It's her age. Cindy too. They're bullying you into giving Richard up. It's not fair.

And what about you? Mum asked then. How come you've suddenly stopped seeing Bob?

I sat back on my heels, surprised.

You thought I hadn't noticed, didn't you? she said

Well...

Did you have a row with him, or is it just that you feel things are muddled too?

Well...

I was a bit feeble, I have to admit. All I could say was well, all the time. I nodded, though.

You see, Mum went on, sometimes when life gets too muddled for us, the way we cope is to tighten things up, get rid of anything that is extraneous to what are really and truly the most important things in our lives, and then we can see more clearly. Extra baggage only weighs us down in situations like this.

Sometimes I worry that Mum takes all that guidance stuff a bit too seriously. Extra baggage? Had I been seeing Bob as extra baggage? I just shook my head while Mum made this little speech. I didn't want to recognise myself in this.

Come on, she said then, a change in her tone, I've got some lupins to divide. Will you help me?

You know I hate lupins, I said.

I know you do, Mum said. But for me?

When you put it like that, I said, what can I say?

Sunday 27th July

Yesterday was one hell of a day. It was my turn to empty the bins, and I was just doing it, going from room to room with my refuse sack, turning all the wastebins upside down into it. But then I found something terrible. I got a dreadful shock. Alva is only just fourteen, after all. I had to sit on the edge of the bath, because my legs were trembling. It was a pregnancy-testing kit, or rather the empty packet of one, in the bathroom bin. The first thing I thought of was that evening when Bob and I drank the loving cup of 'mead'. We drank to fertility. I didn't like the idea at the time, but it was me I was concerned about; I never thought it could happen to Alva. I tore the packet up into tiny pieces and wrapped it in toilet paper before putting it in the refuse sack. I don't know why I did that.

I lay awake half the night, worrying about Alva. She is far too young for this. How could she be so stupid? And after the way she has been brought up, too. Mum has always been so careful to be absolutely open and clear about these things. It's not as though she didn't know, as though she hadn't been told often enough about the consequences of irresponsible behaviour. And there was I thinking that she didn't know what she was talking about when she said she was going to a rave! Maybe she's been to raves before. Maybe she's in with a crowd that take E, or smoke dope, or drink, or anything. God knows what she gets up to when she's off with those friends of hers. They look innocent enough, nice girls, especially Sarah. But you never can tell, I suppose.

Not that there is any point in worrying about all that now. The damage is done. The thing to think about now is how we are all going to cope with this. How is Alva going to get through this? She's only a child. She'll be devastated, physically and emotionally. Oh my god!

My head was in a spin all night. I didn't know what to do. Should I speak to Alva first, or would that freak her out? Or should

I tell Mum, and let her deal with it? Would that be betraying Alva? Well, Mum will stick by her anyway. We both will. We'll all bring it up together. It will be like another little sister. Or a little brother.

That reminded me of Gavin, and I started to cry then. I've never felt so confused. I need to talk it over with someone. I wish I could talk to Bob about it. He's so sane.

I suppose I could.

I think I will.

I'll ring him, I decided, the first moment I get the house to myself. Then I went to sleep.

Monday 28th July

Bob answered the phone himself. I gabbled the whole story at him, at high speed, and he just listened. That's a very helpful thing to do in real life, but over the phone it's quite disconcerting. You keep thinking the other person has gone or you've been cut off or something. I kept stopping to say hello? hello? are you still there?

But he was still there. At the end of it – I told him everything, all about Dad arriving in the middle of the night, Mum going out with Richard, Alva working in the bookshop, Cindy being so awful, what I found in the bin, everything – he said um.

Bob! I practically screamed at him. Is that the best you can manage? Um?

I'm thinking, Ashling, he said. He didn't even sound exasperated. I would have been exasperated with me if I were he.

Oh Bob, I do love you, I said then, and I did, just at that moment, for the way he just said um so thoughtfully, for the way he didn't get exasperated.

What? What did you say, Ashling? What did you say?

He sounded very excited.

Well, I was just saying how I'd wrapped the thing up in loo paper...

No, no, about me, about me, Ashling.

About you saying um?

Yes, yes.

And about how I love you for the way you say it?

That's it, yes. That's it. Boy!

Nobody says Boy! any more, I said. You sound like a Cliff Richard movie.

Wow! he said then. Ah jaysus, fuck-it, he practically roared down the phone. Wow!!

Bob! Watch your language. You're on the phone. Anybody might be listening.

Paranoid as usual, Ashling. But sorry about the language. Are you on your own?

Of course I am. You don't think I'd be telling you all this if there were people around. Mum and Alva have gone to the garden centre.

Right then, I'm coming over. Don't go away. But just while I'm getting there, has it occurred to you that you only found a *package*. The test might have been negative. OK? Bye now. And don't move. I'll be there in fifteen minutes.

Of course it hadn't occurred to me. Bob is so rational. Maybe it wasn't so bad after all. Maybe it *had* been negative. Still, I thought, it's pretty bad that your fourteen-year-old sister *needs* a pregnancy kit, even if it turns out that she isn't pregnant. Pretty damn awful. I mean, you see documentaries about these things, but you don't think it will happen in *your* family.

Bob was here in less than fifteen minutes. He knocked at the door. He always does that. The doorbell in their house is broken, has been for years, so he has got into the habit of knocking instead of ringing. The sound of his knock was like music. I didn't answer immediately. I wanted to hear him knocking again. But as soon as he knocked a second time, I realised it was cruel not to answer, so I flew to the door and flung it open. He had a huge bunch of dog daisies in his hand. I adore dog daisies. I can't imagine how he managed to pick so many in such a short time. He thrust them at me. For the woman who loves me, he said.

Is that not supposed to be for the woman I love? I asked with a laugh.

Steady on, he said. We have established that you love me. I have made no such declaration.

Yet, I said. Come here and give us a kiss.

Well, everyone knows what a kiss is like, so I won't describe it, but it was pretty good.

Then we had a long, long chat. I filled him in on the details about what's been going on in this family since we last spoke, I mean, since we last had a proper talk, not counting tense conversations in the bookshop. Then I asked him what did he think I should do about Alva.

He put his teacup down at this point and he said, Ashling, you've been telling me all sorts of things, but you have never once mentioned that Alva has a boyfriend.

Well, she must have, obviously. I suppose we'll have to get him in on this too. And his parents, oh dear. I hadn't thought of that.

No, not necessarily. She may not *have* a boyfriend.

You mean it might have been a one-night stand? Oh god, Bob, that's worse, I said.

Well, yes, there is that possibility, but let's not get carried away.

Let's look at the facts. We don't know that Alva is pregnant. We don't know that Alva has had the opportunity to get pregnant. We don't know whether the test was positive or negative. All we know is that you found this packet. We don't even know that it was used at all. It might have been a free sample. It might have been a dare. It might have been a joke. Somebody might have picked it up on the street.

And come home and put it in the *bathroom* bin?

Well, no, that doesn't seem very likely, but we don't know that it belonged to Alva.

Well, who else...

Exactly, he said, looking very steadily at me.

Oh Bob!

It began to dawn on me who else might have used it.

Oh god, Bob!

I started to cry then, with the shock of the realisation, I suppose. I cried and cried. My shoulders were shaking, my whole body seemed to go into spasms of sobs. Bob patted my back desperately and pulled my hair out of my eyes. He covered my face with kisses, and he murmured, Stop, Ashling, hush, hush, stop. I didn't mean to upset you. Stop crying, hush.

But I went on crying and crying through it all. When at last I'd finished, and blown my nose several times and wiped my face, Bob said: I'm sorry, I didn't mean it, that was a dreadful thing to say.

You didn't say anything, Bob. You just made me think.

I didn't mean to be insulting. I can't imagine what made me say that.

It's not insulting. It's just a mess.

It's still possible that it is Alva. He said it as if that would be better.

No. It's Mum. She's been sick in the mornings. One morning she was too sick to get up. Oh Bob!

I could feel tears starting to well up again. I felt as if my whole world had split open, as if nothing was in the right place any more, as if I was the only thing in it that stayed in the same place, that everything else was heaving and bubbling around me.

Well, if it's your mum, she'll tell you in her own time, won't she? It's not the end of the world. She's been pregnant before. She can cope.

But she's broken it off with Richard! Oh, this is all such a mess!

That may have been before she knew.

Yes. She must have had an inkling, though.

But she didn't know.

We still don't know, either. It could have been negative, as you said. And there's still an outside chance it could be Alva, I suppose. What'll I do, Bob?

I can't imagine really why I expected Bob to be able to tell me. He's only eighteen, after all, and he hasn't much more experience of life than I have, except that you always think blokes have more experience than we do, even if they don't. But he was the only one I could think of that I could discuss this with. Fidelma, my best friend from school, is away in the south of France with her family, and anyway, I don't think Fidelma would be any use in a situation like this. I don't suppose anybody would be really, except a person's mother, and in this case, that didn't apply.

Sit tight is my advice, said Bob. Let her tell you when she's ready.

But if it's Alva?

You don't really believe that any more, do you? She's a bit naive, but she has her head screwed on, and if she did do something stupid, you'd be the first person she'd turn to, right?

I suppose so.

Just wait and see, Ashling. Sit it out for a bit. It may all come to nothing. Try not to worry about it so much. She's a grown-up. She's come through bad times and got over it.

But for some reason I kept seeing an image in my mind of poor little Gavin, with his dungarees pulled on over his pyjamas and his fist in his mouth.

Cheer *up*, Ashling. I'll make a fresh pot of tea, will I? Nothing like tea in a crisis, is there?

How could I ever have been mean to Bob? And there hasn't been a word of protest from him. Prince Charming he may not be, but he's one of the good guys, that's for sure. Extra baggage! What a terrible thing to say about him.

He's taking me to see *Sense and Sensibility* on Monday. He says I must see it, and he doesn't mind sitting through it again. Isn't that noble of him? Isn't he just the sweetest, kindest, most supportive person? Also, I love the way his hair curls over the top of his shirt collar.

Tuesday 29th July

Mum got a phone call in the middle of the night last night. At least, it was about one o'clock. We were all asleep. I shot awake as soon as I heard the phone. It seemed to be ringing in my heart. I mean it literally seemed like that. My heart seemed to go bleep-bleep, bleep-bleep in my chest cavity. My head felt wild as I sat up on my elbows, my dreams still chasing around in the dark corners of my room, and my heart bleeping like a pacemaker in a magnetic field.

Gavin! was my first thought. Dad and Gavin. Well, that was a natural conclusion. That's who last woke us up in the middle of the night.

The phone was still trilling away hysterically. It seemed much louder in the night than it does in the daytime. I sprang out of bed as if it was an emergency – for all I knew it was – and ran downstairs. We haven't got an upstairs phone. Alva is always going on about it, saying Mum should have one in her room. I'm beginning to see her point. I could hear Mum's door opening as I got to the bottom of the stairs, but I ploughed on, desperate to stop the noise. I was sure the neighbours would start pounding on the walls.

Richard! I gasped, when I heard his voice. Is anything wrong?

Alva? he said in a chuckly voice.

It's Ashling. Is anything wrong?

No, of course not. Is your mum there? I'm on a phone card and this phone is gobbling up the units.

On a phone card? Why? Where are you? Are you sure everything is all right?

Lisbon, he said, less chuckly now. Will you get Margaret please?

Lisbon!

Hurry up, Ashling!

By now Mum was behind my shoulder, shivering in the cold of the hall at night. I handed the phone to her without a word. Then I ran upstairs and pulled the duvet off her bed, and I lumbered down again with it, and tucked it in around her as she sat there, hugging the phone to her collar bone and murmuring into it. Thanks, she mouthed. I noticed a pink streak along her cheek, where her she had been sleeping on a stray strand of hair.

I plodded back up the stairs to bed, but I couldn't get back to sleep. My heart was still racing. After a moment I heard the click as Mum put the phone down, and then I heard another, softer sound, like the phone being picked up again, and the whirring in the ringer that meant she was dialling. She dialled twelve or thirteen numbers. Long distance. She must have been phoning him back, in Lisbon. She was ages. A good fifteen minutes.

This is going to cost a fortune, I thought. I started to do sums in my head, trying to work out how much it would cost, but I didn't have any figures to start with, so it was a bit of a how-long-is-a-piece-of-string exercise. But still my brain kept trying to do the sum. Suppose it's 12p a unit, and suppose a unit to Lisbon is fifteen seconds, that's..., no, let's suppose a unit to Lisbon is five seconds, but it's at a low-rate time, so let's say it's seven seconds, now multiply seven by... what will I multiply it by?

My head was whirling with these irrelevant, pointless calculations, and I had to make a conscious effort to stop myself. As soon as I did, my brain started to work on what she must be saying to him. She had to be telling him. Otherwise she'd never ring him back and stay on for so long. She's careful about the phone.

After what seemed hours, I heard the phone clicking again, and soon afterwards I heard Mum's weary step on the stairs.

Mum? I called out, hoping she'd come in and we could have a chat.

Go to sleep, Ashling, she said firmly.

I heard her door closing, and the muffled sounds of her getting back into bed. My head felt like a concrete block on the pillow.

This morning, she overslept again. This time I didn't go in to check her out. I knew what it was. I had a quick breakfast myself, and then I made her a cup of tea.

We're out of Earl Grey, I said, leaving the cup down beside her and opening the curtains.

Oh, Ashling? she said, opening her eyes and blinking. I must have overslept. The phone call. It was very late.

Overslept? I said. Oh, I thought maybe you weren't well.

She didn't reply.

Are you OK, Mum? I asked, turning back to look at her as I left the room.

She still didn't reply, but there were tears running down her cheeks.

Wednesday 30th July

Mum was in the garden when I got home this evening, kneeling on her little garden hassock and wearing her gardening gloves. She even has a special gardening apron with slots for her trowel and so on. People give her that sort of thing for Christmas.

I brought her an iced soft drink. It was one of those lovely long summer evenings, still warm but with that evening feeling about it, the birds getting twittery and the sun sending out long yellow slants of light. We sat at a little cast-iron table we have on our lawn, under a walnut tree. I asked her how she was feeling, and whether she thought she should be doing all that bending and stretching. I tried to make it sound genuinely concerned, but she must have caught an edge of something knowing or judgmental or sarcastic in my voice in spite of myself.

She put her hand up to her face to shade it from the sun and looked at me and said quietly: You know, Ashling, don't you?

I said I did.

She was silent for a long time then, and I thought she was thinking what to say next, that she was going to launch into a long justification, and I was embarrassed, waiting for her to break the silence. But when she did speak, it was to ask something quite incomprehensible: Was it the eau de cologne?

What? I was really stumped by this one. The eau de cologne? What eau de cologne? What about it?

I can't bear any sort of chemical smells, she said, like perfumes or strong soaps or washing powder, in the early months. They make me sick, make my skin all come up in goose-pimples. I thought that might have been it, how you'd guessed, when I asked you to get rid of the eau de cologne.

The way she said 'in the early months' gave me a creepy feeling. It made the whole thing seem so real, an actual physical and medical reality, whereas up to now I had been regarding it as an emotional problem, a family issue, something whose consequences had to be discussed. She, on the other hand, had already slipped into pregnant woman mode. She would be talking about scans and EDDs and backache and pelvic floor exercises before I knew where I was. (I know all the jargon. Our house is full of pregnancy manuals, along with the personal development books. Also books on holistic healing, herbal medicine, aromatherapy, Bach flower remedies, homeopathy, shiatsu – you name it.)

The pregnancy wasn't just a point of discussion for Mum any longer. It had taken on a life of its own. I remember thinking those very words, and then I suddenly realised how that was literally true. A life of its own. It wasn't just a pregnancy, something related to a pregnancy kit in the bathroom. Here was the start of a life. There was going to be a baby.

Oh Mum! I suddenly wailed, and threw myself into her arms. We hugged very tightly then, not saying anything. I wondered if I should say congratulations. But I just whispered Oh Mum!

several times into her ear. Each time I said it, she just hugged me tighter.

Well, she said, releasing me, *was* it the eau de cologne?

No, no, it wasn't that, I said. It was...

But then I stopped. I couldn't possibly tell her I'd seen the packet in the bin. It was just too undignified. And I certainly couldn't tell her that I had thought it was Alva, or that I had discussed it with Bob. She would die of mortification.

Come on, Mum, I said then, in a jolly tone. How could I possibly have known that eau de cologne has that effect on you? The last time you were pregnant I was what? – three!

We both laughed a small laugh at that, and then we just sat for a long time and sipped our lemonade. We didn't talk much, just enjoyed the garden and the evening. When we'd finished our drinks, I said I'd start the dinner.

She reached out then and pushed my hair back from my forehead and tucked it behind my ears, the way she used to when I was little. That was all.

Can I ask Bob around later? I asked.

Ask him to dinner, she said. Alva won't be here. He can have hers.

Alva was at Sarah's again. This time she'd taken her sleeping bag and was staying over. When Alva and Sarah get together in Sarah's house they go on cleaning binges. They clean the bath and the cooker and the fridge and they wash the floors. It's a sort of playing house, I think. No wonder Sarah's mother loves Alva to come over. They never do it in our house. I don't know why.

We had a lovely evening, just the three of us. I made a big bowl of pasta with garlic and olive oil, and a big bowl of salad, and we took it into the garden, and ate under the walnut tree. Afterwards we had strawberries that Bob brought. We talked about gardening and music and films and food, nothing at all to do with real life. It was lovely, like a little interlude in reality.

Bob had to go early, because he'd arranged to meet a friend back at his house. He was going to show him how to use the Internet, I think. He asked me to come too, and I really wanted to. I wanted to be with him, to saunter down the road with him in the evening light, with our fingers interlaced, and also I wanted to see this famous Internet. But I said no, another time.

When we were washing up, I asked Mum when Richard was due home. She didn't answer, just stood there watching the washing-up water swirling down the plughole. Then she said: Come on, let's go for a walk, just around the block, before it gets too dark.

Friday 1st August

Today was my last day in the bookshop. I'm really going to miss it. I enjoyed it, and it was nice to have extra money for things too, though I saved most of it. The people in the shop sent out for doughnuts at eleven o'clock – I think they've got the idea that I love doughnuts, because I bought them one day – and one of the staff made a pot of real coffee, and we had a little party in Mr George's office, and he ceremoniously handed me my last pay packet and gave me a peck on the cheek and said I'd been a star worker. Nobody ever called me a star before, any kind of star.

Friday 15th August

Bob's Leaving results came out yesterday. He's done very well, by normal standards, but he hasn't done well enough to get into pharmacy, which is what he really wants to do, so he's disappointed. It seems so unfair, because almost anyone else with results as good as his would be over the moon.

Some of them thought they could jump over it anyway. We went into town, and wandered around Temple Bar. The pubs were bulging, people were spilling out onto the streets, and there were people everywhere who were out of their heads, on wild drinking binges. But Bob just didn't feel like celebrating. I bought him (at least, I got Mum to buy him) one of those little bottles of champagne, the ones that only hold one glass, like you get on aeroplanes, but he didn't even open it. He's just down. It's such a shame, because his results were really great – two A's and a string of B's. Some of those idiots who were running riot in town last night probably had a quarter the number of points that he had, and they were obviously delighted with themselves. It seemed crazy that we were so glum about such excellent results. In the end, we just had a hamburger and came home and had an early night.

Thursday 21st August

Mum's invited Richard and Cindy to lunch on Sunday week.

I thought you'd bust up with him! Alva said.

Well, yes, we had agreed to stop seeing each other for a while, Mum said carefully. And he went away for a bit, on a holiday. But we stayed friends.

Friends! snorted Alva.

Yes, said Mum, evenly, and we kept in touch, by telephone, and then I decided I thought I would like to see him again, after all.

Oh, you decided, did you? said Alva, really cheekily.

Alva, Mum said, very firmly, very calmly, I am very sorry if you don't like Richard, or if you don't like my seeing him, but there are things involved here that you don't know anything about.

Such as? Alva was still defiant.

Alva, Alva, Mum said. You can't ask people about things that are private. You know that. There are public aspects to my relationship with Richard, of course. There are you two girls to consider. And Cindy. But you will have to accept, Alva, that I have to make my own decisions about these matters, taking all sorts of things into account, and whether you like my decisions or not, I want you to know that I don't make them lightly, and when I do make decisions I make them carefully, and with regard to all our happiness.

Oh lord, said Alva. Spare me the lecture. Save it for your pupils. And anyway, you *don't* consider all our happiness. I hate Richard. I hate Cindy. I don't want to have anything to do with them. I'm going to live with Daddy!

There was a silence after she said that, a silence like a stone, huge, immoveable, solid.

After what seemed a long, long time, Mum said: Alva, you can't go to your father. The arrangement is that you live with me.

Alva looked miserable, sitting there, staring at her plate. She was dry-eyed, and she didn't shout her next words. It was as if she was squeezing them out: I don't care about your old arrangement. If I want to live with Dad, you're not going to stop me.

No, Alva, I wouldn't stop you, if that was what you really wanted, and if I felt your father could look after you, and if that would be best for your happiness. But it wouldn't work out, love. It wouldn't, and you'd be more miserable than ever.

Well, then, why don't you stop making me miserable, so I can stay here?

I'm not trying to make you miserable. I'm trying to do what's best for all of us. Look, you needn't be at the lunch if it upsets you that much. I'll ring your dad and see if you can go over there on Sunday.

Yes, OK, do that, Alva said quietly. But you are not trying to do what's best for all of us. You are just doing what *you* want.

That's enough, Alva, Mum snapped. I've had enough now, do you hear? I've tried to explain that there are factors here that you don't understand, but you don't seem to be prepared to listen to that. Now, I've said you can go to your dad for that day, and that is the end of this discussion. Right?

Saturday 23rd August

Mum told Alva today, about the baby, I mean. I was upstairs in my room, practising. I'm trying to catch up on all the practice I missed out on while I was working in the shop. I heard Alva thundering up the stairs and her bedroom door banging. I didn't take much notice, because she flies into rages all the time, these days. But when I came down to lay the table for Mum, whose turn it was to cook today, I found her (Mum, I mean) sitting completely still at the end of the table, not crying, not doing anything, just staring, with a concentrated look on her face. I knew then that the row with Alva must have been serious.

She sighed when I asked her what the matter was, and started to talk: I rang Philip (that's my dad) about Alva's going over there next week, and he said he couldn't possibly have her, that Naomi's nerves are in shreds and Alva drives her up the wall, and anyway Gavin has chickenpox. That part's just an excuse. He'll be better by next weekend, but I didn't argue. It was clear that he just doesn't want her. I had to tell Alva she couldn't go. She

72

was furious, of course, and then she started on again about how I shouldn't be seeing Richard anyway, and how much she hated Cindy and Richard, and how I wasn't taking her happiness into account. So in the end, I had to tell her about the baby. She said terrible things to me, and then she banged out of the room. Oh Ashling!

I'll talk to her, I said.

I went up to her room, and tried the door, but she'd locked it. I could hear her crying behind it. I rattled and knocked, and eventually she let me in, when she realised it wasn't Mum. I sat on the edge of the bed and rocked her in my arms, and then we talked and talked, for ages, about all sorts of things, not about Mum and Richard and the baby at all, but about school, and clothes, and television programmes, all sorts of things. I brushed her hair for her, and we tried it in different styles, but it's quite bushy, like Mum's. It didn't look right tied up or in pigtails, and in the end, we put it back the way it always was. She asked me to make her up, but I don't wear makeup, except lipstick, but she said that would do, so I went and got three colours, and she tried them all on, and then she used one of the lipsticks, which is a sort of a brownish colour, as eyeshadow. It sounds daft, but it worked. She looked nice.

We talked about boys, then, and she told me about a secret passion she had had for a boy in third year, Aidan, who's a rollerblade champion, but that it had worn off when she discovered he liked Blur. I laughed at that, but she is committed to Oasis, as well as Boyzone, and it seems that anyone who is for Oasis has to be against Blur. I never knew that. It's all just pop music to me. And anyway, she went on, he supports *Everton*. She practically spat that bit out. It seems to be the greatest offence

73

of all. And he's tone deaf, she added.

Which presumably explains why he's for Blur? I concluded.

No, that's not true, she said, very fairly, I thought. It hasn't got anything to do with their music. You're just for one or the other, that's all. But being tone deaf means he doesn't understand real music. Not like we do. If he knew I played the flute, he'd probably think that was silly or affected or something.

Not half as silly as the double-bass, though, I said.

We lay on our stomachs then, across her bed, and waved our feet at the ceiling, and Alva asked me about Bob, and why I'd broken off with him, and why I'd got back together with him. I said I didn't really know why I'd broken with him, that I had felt confused, and that I got back with him because I missed him, which is true, but not the whole truth. Then she told me she thought she'd never have a boyfriend because she isn't pretty enough. That made me feel really wretched, after what I'd been thinking about her and the pregnancy kit.

I told her that in the first place she is pretty, which she is, and that secondly, even though being pretty undoubtedly has something to do with it, it isn't really the main thing, and people get together for all sorts of reasons, and that anyway, lots of fourteen-year-olds feel like that, and they usually end up married by the time they're twenty-five. And anyway, I added, very wisely, having a boyfriend is not the most important thing.

It is, she answered. It's OK for you to say that, you've got Bob. And look at Mum. She couldn't last without one, and now look at the situation *she's* in. It *is* important, Ashling. I know it shouldn't be the most important thing, that there's music, and God, and being kind to children and old people, and saving the environment, and getting involved with your community, and study, and careers, but none of those things will *do*.

I suppose she's right. Sort of. I know that shouldn't be so. But it does seem to matter terribly, doesn't it?

Monday 1st September

School has started. I'm in my final year, now, and everyone is telling us it's terribly important to work hard this year. Bob's going to college next month, to study engineering.

I'm beginning to agree with Alva that Cindy really is unbearable. I gave her the benefit of the doubt the first time, but she was insufferable yesterday. At least she dressed decently this time. In fact she overdid it a bit. She had her hair all piled up in an elaborate style, and her makeup would make you run for a facecloth. And she hung onto her father's arm as if she owned him. She looked around our living room as if she was buying the house, and was trying to convey that she didn't think much of it, to keep the price down. I felt I should be running around plumping up cushions and hiding things she mightn't approve of. But she seemed to disapprove of everything. 'Haughty' is the only word I can think of.

Poor Mum looked very strained, all through the meal. Richard tried to make her have a glass of wine. He should know better, in her condition. Alva and I were delighted to get out to the kitchen to do the washing up. I was terrified Cindy was going to offer to come with us to help, to give Mum and Richard a chance to be alone for a little while, but she didn't. I don't know whether she knows about the baby, and if she doesn't it would be dreadful if Alva blurted it out.

I brought the coffee in, and there was silence in the dining room. It wasn't just that people weren't talking. It was as if they'd

75

never even met each other. It was the sort of silence you might get in a doctor's waiting room, full of strangers with nothing to say to each other. I suggested Monopoly, to break the ice more than anything. Cindy's eyes lit up, like a small child's. Good, I thought, I've hit on something that she likes.

You can be banker, Alva said to Cindy, very generously, I thought, as she unfolded the board.

She was banker and she cheated. We could all see her at it, but she did it just the same. She won hands down, naturally. We were glad to see them go.

Tuesday 2nd September

Alva bought me a present yesterday. I was doing my homework in my room and she came in with her eyes all shining, saying she had bought me something really special. She said it was an unbirthday present, and it was to thank me for putting up with her lately. I was delighted. I thought it might be a box of Roses or something like that. But it was a poster of Boyzone, identical to the one she has in her own room! Alva was so pleased with herself that I couldn't disappoint her by appearing to be unimpressed. I thanked her profusely and propped the rolled-up poster against my chest of drawers, hoping she would go away and forget all about it, but she arrived back in a few moments with a packet of blu-tack and insisted on putting it up herself, right over my bed. She even took down the reproduction of Monet's water-lilies that I had there, and put it on the opposite wall. Oh well, at least I don't have to look at Boyzone while I'm in bed, and it's rather nice to have the water-lilies on the opposite wall, where I can enjoy them before I go to sleep.

My head feels like a fizz-bag this evening. It began with Alva saying she hoped Mum wasn't going to *marry* Richard.

I said I thought that wasn't very likely, at least not for the present. I said that Mum didn't approve of people getting married just because they are pregnant. Alva said that was young people. She said older people made different rules for themselves and for young people. She said wouldn't it be awful to have the noxious Cindy for a sister.

When she said that I felt as if I'd been stabbed. Not stabbed, exactly. It wasn't a sharp feeling. More as if I'd been thumped, maybe, but hard. She'd only be a stepsister, I said at last, and as I said it I realised I was gasping.

Yes, but we'd all have to live together, Alva said.

Oh come on, Alva, I said, trying to act cheerful. Don't go looking for trouble. There is no evidence whatsoever that they are thinking about getting married. Look on the bright side. Think about the baby. Won't it be lovely?

It might look like Cindy, Alva said gloomily.

I hadn't thought about that. I hadn't thought of the baby as being related to Cindy. I had imagined it as belonging to us, just us three. I suppose I had imagined Richard sort of hovering benignly in the background, but not Cindy. I hadn't reckoned on Cindy.

The idea that the baby would be related to Cindy made me feel very strange. It was like when you are watching a film, and there's a spooky bit, and they play spooky music, a chromatic scale or something, so you know it's something spooky. I felt as if my mother had an alien child growing inside her. That made me want to wrap myself up in my own family and exclude everyone else.

Poor Bob. I know I have been very unfair on him, breaking up with him twice in the space of a few weeks, but I had exactly the same feeling when I thought about Cindy and the baby that I got that night in the bowling alley. I felt out of place and claustrophobic and confused all at the same time, and I felt I just couldn't cope with anyone outside of me, Mum and Alva. So I rang Bob up after I'd finished my homework and asked him to come out for a walk.

We walked around our housing estate, trying to talk. We kept meeting people out with their dogs or going for a run or calling their children in for bed, and they all wanted to stop and talk. I think the neighbours know something is going on in our family and are trying to find out what it is. They don't usually want to engage me in long heart-to-hearts about the weather. We met Joan Merrigan, hurrying back from the local shops with one of those long narrow paper bags they put wine in, only I think it was gin, and she stopped and asked very particularly after Mum, and gave me a deep, meaningful look. Maybe that's not true. Maybe it was just Joan being her usual breathy, over-wrought self. Am I going paranoid or what?

Anyway, in between all these interruptions, I tried to explain it all to Bob, how I felt, but this time he was angry as well as upset, and I felt I deserved his anger. He said I had used him as an emotional prop when things had got too much for me – and I couldn't argue with that. It was true. I had. But I said it would be dishonest to go on using him, and if I didn't break up with him now, that's what I would be doing. He didn't seem to see it that way, but he didn't argue any more. He walked back with me as far as my gate without another word. Then he said good night very curtly and walked quickly away, without even a token kiss. I thought something inside me was going to burst as I watched his back receding down the cul-de-sac. I wanted to call out that I was sorry and would he please come back, but I knew that if I did that I'd only do the same again in another few weeks. I knew for sure this time that I just couldn't cope with my relationship with Bob on top of everything else in my life. But I felt very sad, and I wanted to cry, but tears wouldn't come.

Saturday 6th September

Well, Alva was right and I was wrong. Mum and Richard are engaged! Mum even has a ring. She showed it to us yesterday. It's a very narrow band of white gold, with several tiny diamonds studded into it, very pretty and very understated. But she is keeping it in its little velvet box in a drawer in her room, because it's not 'official' yet. It seems pretty official to me, if there's a ring, but I think when she says it's not official what she means is that Cindy doesn't know.

Alva didn't say anything when Mum showed us the ring. I tried to say something enthusiastic, but I don't know if it came out right. Afterwards, Alva said to me that she hopes Cindy will go away to university soon. She means that if Mum and Richard get married, we'll all have to live together. There's not much room here, so presumably we will have to go and live with them. I'd hate that. I grew up in this house. I'm fond of it. It's home.

But I told Alva there wasn't much chance of Cindy moving out of home, just for our convenience. I tried to get her to see it from Cindy's point of view. I said we would all have to put up with the situation, and that maybe we would get on much better when we knew each other better. Alva just tapped the table when I said all

79

this, and listened with her eyebrows raised. Sometimes I could shake her, she is so exasperating.

But if I'm honest, I have to say that the best thing about this engagement is the ring. That's really not a very cheering thought.

I heard Alva crying in her room again last night.

Tuesday 9th September

I've just had an awful thought. Suppose Alva decides to go and live with Dad? Or rather, decides she *wants* to go and live with him. He wouldn't have her. He wouldn't even have her for a day that time she wanted to go over there to avoid having to meet Richard. I hope she doesn't even think of it, because she would be devastated if he said no.

Friday 12th September

I went into Mum's room in my dressing gown last night, before I went to bed. She was already in bed, reading a detective story. It was very difficult in the beginning. I couldn't very well start by saying, Well, Mum, this engagement of yours is the problem. But of course she knew, she always knows. She put down her book, patted a spot near the edge of the bed for me to sit on, and started by saying: I am sure my engagement to Richard is difficult for you, Ashling.

I sat down with a bump and said: Oh no, no, of course not. It's Alva.

But of course it wasn't just Alva.

Mum sighed that special quality of sigh she reserves for matters concerning Alva, and she said: It's partly *because* of Alva that we are getting married.

Well, that really takes the biscuit, I thought.

Because of *Alva*! I yelped.

Mum smiled slightly and said: Yes, I know, it sounds ridiculous. I know Alva thinks this is pure selfishness.

Oh no, no, I cut in loyally, but Mum put up a hand to stop me and went on.

Look Ashling, I can tell you what's going on, because you are older and more mature, but you are not to tell this to Alva, right?

I couldn't answer. It was as if my tongue had grown into the roof of my mouth. What revelation was going to come now? What *more* could there be? I nodded.

You know your father has been going through a bad patch, Mum said.

Dad! What on earth had Dad to do with it?

Well, Mum went on, it's more than a bad patch. I think it's something closer to a nervous breakdown, actually. But whatever it is, he has become extremely agitated about my relationship with Richard. Don't ask how he found out. These things get around, it's a small city. Anyway, he started to threaten me that he would sue me for custody of you two, although I think actually you are old enough in law to make up your mind, it's really Alva this would apply to. I laughed at him at first. But he was dead serious. He said he would have me declared an unfit mother.

My tongue finally broke free of the roof of my mouth and I let out a cry of No, no, Mum!

Mum put a hand up again, and she went on talking, as if she had something she had to get to the end of.

I know, I know, it's ridiculous, and as things stood six months ago, he wouldn't have had a leg to stand on. But if I had a baby, it is just possible that a very conservative judge might agree with him. It's not all that likely, but it is a possibility I have to think about.

But *he* has a baby and *he's* not married, I said.

Mum gave a crooked smile and said: Have you never heard of double standards? And anyway, he's in what's called a 'stable relationship'.

And you're not? I asked, incredulously.

Well, I can't prove it. And I haven't known Richard very long. It just doesn't look good.

I could see her point. It looked terrible, actually, when you thought about it like that.

Look, Mum said, more cheerfully, the chances of his being able to take Alva away from me, from us, are pretty slim, particularly when you consider how unstable he is himself. But I don't want him to be in a position even to start *threatening* something like that. I am not putting this family through that sort of emotional battle. And I am quite sure that if I am safely married off to somebody else, then Philip wouldn't dream of making a fuss. He's like that, old-fashioned.

But Mum, I said, that's not a very good reason for you to marry Richard.

It is, Mum said, it's a very good reason indeed, the best reason I can think of. But I agree that if that was the *only* reason, it would be a very poor basis for a marriage. There is the fact that I love Richard, too. I think that counts for something as well.

I hugged her then and while I hugged her, I whispered, Congratulations! in her ear.

Thanks, she whispered back. Then she said, still in a whisper: You do like Richard, don't you, Ashling?

I nodded. But I had to be honest, so as I drew back, I added:

It's the noxious Cindy I'm concerned about.

Noxious! Mum said, pretending to be shocked.

It's Alva's word for her, I said. And it's accurate.

I'm sorry, love, Mum said then. I'm truly sorry. I know Cindy is a bit of a thorn in the side. But we have to forgive her a lot. It's very hard for her too. And she has just lost her mother. If I could think of a way of doing this without messing you all up, I would. I was prepared to give him up, you know that. But the baby has really put the tin hat on it.

Poor baby, I said. We have to stop thinking about him as a problem. He won't have much of a start in life if we think of him as a stumbling block.

What makes you think it will be a he? Mum asked, with that delighted smile mothers have when people talk about their babies.

I dunno, I said. But I do know. I'm hoping for a little boy, because I don't want yet another new sister – Cindy is quite enough to contend with – but mainly because I am hoping for a little brother like Gavin, only this time, one we can have at home. Poor little Gavin. I hope he's OK.

I had a very strong desire to ring Bob up this morning before school, just to say hi. But I knew that I didn't really just want to say hi. What I really wanted was to tell him all the latest developments and see what he thought. But I can't do that. It wouldn't be fair to him. And anyway, my family life is not a soap opera for relaying in instalments to other people.

Friday 19th September

Well, it's official now. The wedding date has been set for the twentieth of October. Cindy has been told. We didn't put a notice in the paper. I think that would have been fun. Alva and I could have announced it, the way people's parents usually do, but Mum put her foot down. I think she doesn't want Dad finding out until it's all over and done with.

Mum has started to wear her ring, just in the evenings, though, not to school. She's starting to show, just a little. She can't wear those little slimline skirts she usually wears any more. It's all starting to feel more real.

Sunday 28th September

Mum and I went shopping for maternity clothes for her yesterday. The proper maternity shops are way too expensive, so we just went to the department stores instead and looked at dresses in huge sizes. We bought two dresses, one more awful than the other, but Mum insisted that it didn't matter, it was only for a few months. We went for a cup of coffee afterwards (my treat, Mum wouldn't dream of spending money in a café when you could have a perfectly good cup of coffee at home for a quarter of the price). While we were having our coffee, I opened up the bags and shook out the dresses. We had bought them in different weights, one for now, while the weather is still quite mild, in viscose, and one really voluminous one in wool that she can put a few layers under for extra warmth, for when the weather is very cold. Mum keeps saying you don't need to be very warmly dressed when you are pregnant because the baby keeps you warm. I find that very hard to believe. Anyway, the dresses are far too long for Mum, because they are meant for much larger women, so we will have to spend a few nights taking them up. No matter what we do with them, they are going to look ghastly.

As I was looking despairingly at them, it suddenly occurred to me: Mum, I yelped in anguish. You can't possibly get married in one of these!

Why not? Mum asked, unconcernedly.

Because they are hick, they are dowdy, they are perfectly dreadful.

It doesn't matter, Mum said. It's only going to be a registry office wedding, very low key, it doesn't matter what I wear.

Well, I never heard such rubbish. A woman who doesn't care what she looks like on her wedding day!

Think of the photographs, Mum! I said. Think about yourself in twenty years time, looking back at your wedding day. You won't want Fido there to be embarrassed when he looks at his parents' wedding photos.

Wedding photos! Mum said, astonished, as if I had said 'wedding helicopter'.

Yes, Mum, people *take* photographs of these occasions, I said.

Well, we don't have to do that. It's going to be very–

Low key, yes, that's fine, and we don't need to get a professional in or anything, but we have to have at least a few snaps. You have Fido to think about now. It's going to be part of his family history.

Stop calling it Fido, Mum said.

Stop changing the subject, I said. Next week we are coming back into town, and we are going to buy you something decent to wear for your wedding.

No, Ashling, Mum said, please, no.

Just then, Bob appeared beside our table balancing a tray with a teapot and two cups. He was with his friend Gerard. Gerard was carrying a motor-cycle helmet. He must have got a bike.

Hi Ashling, Bob said. Hi, Mrs Magee.

Well, hello, Bob! Mum said, delightedly.

I started to pull the chair next to mine out, for him to sit on, but after he'd said hi, Bob walked on, carrying his tray, and Gerard nodded at the two of us and followed him. They sat at a table miles away, the furthest away table they could find.

Mum looked at me. I don't know how I looked, but I felt like the only child in the class that hasn't been picked for the football team.

Come on, Ashling, Mum said. Let's go.

Wednesday 8th October

There's been a bit of a row about the wedding. I suppose there always is about weddings. Mum wanted me and Alva to be bridesmaids, but Richard said that wouldn't be fair, unless Cindy could be too. Mum said of course Cindy could be, but then Richard said Cindy didn't want to be. So Mum said that was fine, she didn't have to be, that Alva and I would do it. But then Richard said that if Cindy wasn't going to be a bridesmaid, then we shouldn't be either.

But she doesn't *want* to be a bridesmaid, Richard, Mum said.

I know, I know, Richard said. But I still don't think it would be right for Ashling and Alva to do it if Cindy can't.

Won't, Mum said, very sharply.

Isn't, Richard said.

Mum gave in. Alva was furious with her. I said it didn't matter, but Alva said it mattered dreadfully, it was our mother getting married and we were being refused the right to be her witnesses because of a stuck-up, spoilt, noxious bitch.

Mum said Alva was never to say a thing like that again about Cindy, that this was very hard on Cindy, and after all –

86

Yeh, yeh, Alva said, she's recently bereaved and she's in grief, yeh, yeh, I know.

Then she said she would take back the bitch part, but not stuck-up, noxious or spoilt.

Mum let it go at that. Alva said afterwards to me that she only took back the bitch part because it was hard on dogs.

Friday 17th October

Alva is still awfully upset about not being a bridesmaid at the wedding. I think some relations of Richard's are going to be the official witnesses. So I said, why didn't we get two lovely glamorous new outfits, *as if* we were bridesmaids, and we can stand next to Mum in all the photos, and nobody need ever know that we hadn't actually signed the register, which is all that being witnesses really means anyway. Alva said sulkily that she supposed that would do.

I can't imagine where the money is going to come from for two glamorous outfits for me and her, after all the money we spent getting Mum's outfit. Yes, I finally persuaded her not to get married in one of the hideous dresses, and we got her a nice cream silk tunic-blouse and a pair of loose cream woollen trousers with a drawstring. It looks very simple and elegant, but like all simple things it cost an arm and a leg.

Dad gave Mum a string of pearls as a present when they got married and she wore them on their wedding day. They're the only jewellery she has, apart from her fake pearl ear-rings and her engagement ring, so I said she should wear them for the wedding, they would look great with the silk shirt. She said she couldn't possibly do that. I suppose I can see her point. So then she thrust them at me and said: Here, you wear them, Ashling. I can't really own these any more. You have them.

They are a bit old-fashioned for me, but they are lovely all the same. I'll wear them for the wedding, and then I'll put them away until I'm older.

Anyway, the three of us are going into town on Saturday with the Access card, and we're going to get something decent for me and Alva to wear. By the time the Access bill comes, Mum will be married, and I suppose Richard can pay it. It will be nice not to have to worry about money. That's something.

Tuesday 21st October

The wedding was a very short, quick ceremony. Actually, it was more like a procedure. It was disappointingly unceremonious. Cindy didn't show up until it was all over, which I thought was a bit off of her. We went for coffee afterwards, and then we went back to their house, and we were just opening the champagne when she arrived, her face all red and her hair all wild and a big long scarf flying, as if she'd been out in the wind. Well, I suppose she had been. It's that time of year. But she didn't look like a wedding guest. Alva and I got two really nice dresses, in the end. Richard insisted on paying for them. (I didn't tell him we had just been going to put them on the Access bill and hope he'd pay it anyway.) Mine was a deep green silk with a sort of kingfisher blue sheen, with a V-neck at the front and a plunging back, and I wore a blazer over my shoulders, because it wasn't really an October dress. Alva's was a deep rose pink, in a very similar cut. She's warm-blooded, so she managed without a blazer, and she looked very elegant.

The woman who was the bridesmaid is Richard's sister and she doesn't have any arms. He might have told us. It's hard not to stare.

After the wedding meal, which we had at a local Italian restaurant, local to Richard's house, I mean, Richard and Mum went home to Richard's house. Alva went to stay for a few days with Sarah, and I am staying with my friend Fidelma. I don't know what Cindy's doing. I think she's staying somewhere for a while too, to give Mum and Richard a bit of honeymoon time together, just till the weekend.

Our house is going to be put up for sale. Dad doesn't know yet, and we can't put the house on the market until Mum talks to him, I think. That gives us a bit of a breather, and we have an illusion of a home. I mean we still have a doorkey, and most of our things are still there, and we drop in all the time to get stuff we need, but it's more like a stage set now than a home. It feels sort of sad when we go in there. It still smells like home, but it is so silent. Mum will miss the garden. She put so much work into it. And especially the walnut tree; it was her special tree. It never produced any walnuts, of course, but that isn't the point. It's all so sad. It's like the end of my childhood.

Saturday 25th October

Alva and I went home today, to collect some of the things we want to take to Richard's house. We are going to have to start thinking of Richard's house as our house now, but it's hard to do that when our real house is still there, with half of our things still in it. Our pyjamas and toothbrushes and clothes and things are at Richard's already. Mum has been doing lots of little forays in the car in the evenings after school, and she has moved most of the basic necessities already, but I decided I wasn't going without Betsy (my double-bass), and Alva wanted her Boyzone poster, so we met there this morning.

Alva insisted that I would need my Boyzone poster too, so I let her take it, and I took the Monet print down as well. I felt a bit like a thief, which is ridiculous in our own house, with our own things. I jumped when the doorbell rang. I thought it must be the police.

It was Joan, from across the road.

I just thought I'd pop in! she squealed excitedly when I opened the door. Oh this is all so thrilling, Ashling! Isn't your mother the sly one, sneaking off and getting married like that, and nobody any the wiser!

I didn't ask her how she knew. I didn't want to talk to her about it. I felt like slamming the door in her seedy, floozy face, with its madcap-looking halo of fuzzed-up, moussed, dyed hair.

But then she produced an envelope and pressed it into my hand. She said: I was going to buy your mother a wedding present, but I didn't know what to get, because I know she's not exactly setting up home from scratch, it's not like she needs a toaster or a clock or a mugtree, so then I thought I'd give *you* a little present instead, just a little thank-you for all the babysitting, I don't know what I'm going to do without you.

And then she kissed me. It was a rather unpleasant kiss, sort of moist and hurried and lipsticky, and I wanted to wipe it away immediately. My hand went almost automatically to my face, but then I stopped myself. It would have been terribly rude to wipe the kiss away in front of her. That wasn't the only reason I stopped, though. As soon as my fingers reached my cheeks they touched wet, and I realised I was crying. I don't exactly know why.

I nodded my thanks at her and shut the door. There was a cheque for thirty-five pounds in the envelope. When I saw that, I cried even harder.

Alva came downstairs carrying swathes of muslin.

What's that, Alva? I asked, wiping my face. Where are you going with all that stuff?

Our mosquito nets, remember?

I did remember then. When we were small children Mum did up our rooms for us, and she hung mosquito nets over our beds, for decoration, because we were going through a phase of playing princesses, and they gave a sort of four-poster effect. They were rather pretty. I hadn't seen them for years. They never went back up after the rooms were repainted when we got older.

I found them in the hot press, Alva said. I thought it would be nice to take them to Richard's, for our room.

I thought it was a ridiculous notion, silly and sentimental, and anyway they had got yellow and tatty by now, but I could see Alva was quite charmed by the idea (I think sometimes she's still stuck in the princesses phase), so I helped her to fold them up and put them in a holdall.

Mum must have had a similar, but more practical idea, because when we got to Richard's house, there they all were, Mum and Richard and Cindy, having tea in the kitchen, and there was our old chequered tablecloth from home on the table. We got it in France one year, when Alva and I were children, and we've used it and used it, and it's still almost as bright as ever. It was like a little piece of my childhood here now in this new house. I was very touched by it. I'm sure Mum did it on purpose, as a sort of little welcome for us. She poured us tea from Richard's teapot, and we sat down and ate barm brack (Alva's favourite type of cake, good old Mum) off our old tablecloth and talked politely to Richard and Cindy, telling them all about the trouble we had getting Betsy on the bus.

They laughed at that. It was nearly like being a family. The tablecloth definitely helped.

Monday 27th October

It's all a bit fraught around here, but I suppose that is only to be expected. The house is quite large, but Alva and I seem to have got the smallest room. Mum says they are going to do a job on the attic soon, and we will have a new room up there. I think Cindy is jealous. She would like to have been offered the attic instead of us, but I am quite sure if she had been, and we were to get her old room, she would have been even more miffed. She's determined to be injured, no matter what happens.

Meanwhile, we have our own washbasin which helps. There's a queue for the bathroom in the mornings. I think Cindy stays in there deliberately long, to keep us late. It's tough on Mum, who needs the bathroom more often than the rest of us these days, but she can't very well complain. It's still not really her house.

Wednesday 29th October

It's my birthday soon, my seventeenth, and Mum is insisting I have a big splash. I think she is desperately trying to make up to us for all the stress lately, and she thinks a big posh party will help. I don't want a big posh party, but Mum is so dead-set on it, I'm going along with it. It gives her something to concentrate on apart from Cindy and how badly she is behaving. And she is being a total cow. Alva and I are really trying. At least I am, and I am encouraging Alva to try too. But we are not getting very far. Cindy is like an ice-maiden. She hardly talks to us. It's like being the lodger in a rather stiff boarding house.

Alva still cries in the night, a lot. She waits till she thinks I am asleep, and then she starts. It's dreadful to hear her. Sometimes even the thought of the baby doesn't help.

Sunday 9th November

The birthday party was great. Mum really went to town on it. We had streamers, and a three-piece band, and a disco in the conservatory and punch and a big ice-cream cake, and even a kissogram. I think Mum enjoyed it even more than I did. She was revelling in having a house large enough to throw a big party in. It was her first event as hostess in Richard's house, and that was important to her too. It's a sort of benchmark, I suppose, a statement about who lives here.

I was quite relieved when Cindy said she didn't want to come. I couldn't very well have left her out, now that we all live together. However, she said she was going to her aunt's for the weekend, and she was sorry, she just couldn't make it. Anyway, she said, she didn't have a ballgown. I don't know where on earth she got the idea we were all going to be wearing ballgowns. I had said people were going to dress up a bit, you know, not just come in their old jeans and sweaters, just for the fun of it, but she decided that meant it was a formal affair and she said it wasn't her style.

Of course some people did come in their old jeans and sweaters, but most people made some sort of an effort. Some of the girls coloured their hair, blue and pink and silver, that temporary colour, you know. Others put their hair up and put sparkly stuff in it. Some of them got hold of quite swish dresses, and borrowed stuff from their mothers, jewellery and so on, and high-heels. Alva and I both wore our wedding outfits. They weren't too weddingy, and they worked fine as party dresses. It was a bit of gas, when you are used to seeing people in holey jeans or baggy tracksuits. Even the boys managed ties, if not jackets. One boy had his face painted. It was really great. All sort of silvery and glittery.

I felt a bit sad that Bob wasn't there. I suppose I could have invited him, just for old times' sake, but I thought he might refuse. I couldn't blame him if he did, but I couldn't bear the thought of it either, so I didn't ask him in the end. I still miss him a lot.

Cindy arrived back from her aunt's wearing a pair of outsize novelty slippers that she had borrowed from her aunt. She looked very odd, standing on the doorstep with what looked like two puppy dogs on her feet. She had some daft story about losing one of her shoes at a bus-stop or something. She was lucky it was a dry day, because those slippers would have disintegrated in the rain. We had a bit of a laugh over the slippers. When she drops her guard at a moment like that, when her sense of humour is tickled, she can be almost human. Sometimes, I think we might even get to be friends.

Thursday 20th November

I answered the phone yesterday, and this voice asked to speak to Cindy, a young man's voice. For a second I thought it sounded like Bob, and I said: Hey, is that Bob?

As soon as I said it, I could feel myself blushing like mad. I felt I'd made a complete fool of myself, gushing at a stranger like that on the phone.

There was silence on the other end of the line. Complete silence. Then the person hung up. I shrugged and hung up too. Looper, I thought. Certainly not worth being embarrassed about.

Then the phone rang again, and somebody asked to speak to Cindy. It still sounded a bit like Bob, but the accent was different this time. It sounded German, I think. But even so, I asked: Oh, did you ring just a minute ago?

I didn't feel embarrassed this time. I felt he was the one acting a bit odd. There was this silence again, and then the person said, very cautiously, No? Like that, with a question-mark at the end of it. I said: Well, anyway, Cindy's not in just at the moment. Who should I say was looking for her?

Dr Martin, the voice said, very slowly and articulately. Dok-torr Marr-tin, like that.

He sounded a bit young to be a doctor.

OK, I said, and your number?

Another silence. Then I could hear pages being turned, as though the person was looking for a number. How come this person doesn't know his own number? I thought.

Anyway, he gave me the number eventually, and I wrote it down and I stuck the message up where we leave phone messages for each other. It wasn't all that very strange, really, I suppose, but I felt a bit uneasy, at the way I had jumped to the conclusion it was Bob, just because it sounded his sort of age. He must have a deeper hold on my imagination than I realised. And if it wasn't Bob – and I don't really think it was, that was just a bit of wishful thinking or something on my part – well then why was he behaving so oddly?

There was another message for Cindy today, I think from the same person, in handwriting I didn't recognise. It must have been Richard's, I suppose. This time the message said something about a podiatric appointment. I wonder if Cindy has something wrong with her feet. Maybe that's why she was wearing those funny slippers the other day. Maybe she has corns or something. Poor thing if she does. Cindy and I are getting on much better lately. I think she is beginning to accept the situation. It can't be any easier for her than for us; maybe even harder, actually, when you consider that her home has been invaded.

Sunday 23rd November

What a day this has been! I'd better start at the beginning.

I was practising upstairs in the afternoon. The neighbours around here don't seem to mind when I play. I can get loads of practice done, which is good, because we are having our Christmas concert early this year, and I have a lot of stuff to learn. The only problem is that our room is a bit small for two beds, two wardrobes, two dressing-tables, a double-bass, a stool and a music stand, so it's a bit cramped. I haven't much room for my bowing elbow.

Anyway, the doorbell rang as I was practising. I had just answered the door a few minutes previously, and I'd had to drag a ladder around to lend to the woman next door, who, I am quite convinced, just wanted to get a good look at us. I decided I'd had enough interruptions, and somebody else could answer it this time, so I just went on playing. I heard the door being opened shortly after that, and minutes later I could hear Alva pounding up the stairs. You always know when it's Alva. She has a particular way of pounding. She burst into our room, swinging a black boot by its laces, and shouting Ashling, Ashling, oh Ashling, and she flung herself down on the bed.

I thought the woman next door must have fallen off the ladder and broken her spine at the very least, Alva was so agitated, though I couldn't see where this boot came into it. I noticed it looked like the one Cindy brought home that day when she arrived wearing the doggy slippers.

Alva kept rocking back and forth on the bed and shaking her

head and just saying, Ashling!, so I forgot about the boot, propped Betsy carefully against the wall and grabbed Alva by the wrists and shook her. Alva, I said, come on Alva, spit it out.

It's Bob, Alva whispered.

What is? What about Bob?

At the door, Alva said. Don't go down, Ashling. Don't!

Why ever not? I asked. Don't be so melodramatic, Alva. But how did he know where to find me?

Ashling! Alva squawked, in a half-strangulated voice, as I left the room. Don't go down! It's not for you!

When I got to the top of the stairs, I froze. Bob was in the hall. I could see the top of his head from my vantage point on the landing. I'd know that head anywhere. He had Cindy in his arms and he was kissing her. My dear, sweet, kind old Bob, kissing the noxious Cindy! (Not that I think she's noxious any more. She's just as confused and upset as we are.) I stood and watched. I couldn't help it. It was a long kiss. I thought my heart would burst.

Then it dawned on me that this was the person Cindy had met at the bus-stop. She'd had a daft story about meeting some bloke and losing her boot. And of course it had been Bob who'd rung for Cindy last week, I thought, in that way your mind grabs hold of irrelevant details when you're under stress. He must have been surprised when I answered, that's why there was that long silence. But I don't think that meant he knew I lived here. I could have been just a friend of Cindy's or a neighbour or anything, who happened to answer the phone. I might have been a babysitter, even, if Cindy had younger brothers or sisters. Of course, he couldn't be sure it was me, and he didn't want to ask, but he wasn't taking any chances. That's why he left a codename. That's why he didn't give his own number, either. It must have been a friend's number he used. He knew I'd recognise his, if it really was me. All this fell into place like a jigsaw as I stood and watched that endless kiss.

Then Bob and Cindy broke apart and looked at each other. I felt like a voyeur, standing there. I spun around and went back into my room. Alva was still sitting on the bed. I told you not to go, she kept repeating, I told you, I told you.

My heart was pounding, but I think it was shock. I don't think I felt actively jealous. I don't *think* so.

What's going on, Alva? I asked. Have you been talking to Bob?

Just when I answered the door, Alva said. He got the shock of his life. He's a friend of Cindy's. He said he met her recently, and he had arranged to call around to see her today. I told him we were living here now too. I had to tell him that Mum had married Cindy's father. Oh, Ashling, what are we going to do?

I heard the sitting-room door close. Cindy'd been in there since lunch, lying down, said she felt a bit sick. She must have taken him in.

What we are going to do, Alva, I said, in a very controlled voice, is act dignified.

Oh, Ashling, you're taking this so well, Alva said admiringly.

Am I? I asked. Well, whatever we do, I don't want to embarrass anybody, not Cindy, not Bob, and especially not myself.

At that moment, not embarrassing myself seemed the most important thing in the world, and not embarrassing Bob seemed the next most important thing. I decided I would concentrate on that, and worry about whether I felt jealous later. I knew I wasn't entitled to feel jealous. I'd sent him packing. He was entitled to find somebody else, perfectly entitled.

Look, let's go and talk to Mum, I suggested.

Mum and Richard were in the kitchen, just finishing clearing up after lunch. The dishwasher was humming away, and there were still streaks on the table, where the J-cloth had been swished over it. The kitchen had that freshly washed look about it, all the worktops gleaming, even the taps winking. Richard and Mum were kissing when we opened the door. They grinned when they saw us standing there. They were trying not to look embarrassed.

Alva was hopping from foot to foot, still holding Cindy's wretched boot.

What's got you so worked up, Alva? Mum asked, from Richard's arms. Honestly, this house seemed to be full of kissing couples this afternoon.

Mum went on: Do you want something? Is this a delegation?

Alva went on hopping, and looked at me to speak.

I explained to Mum that a boyfriend of Cindy's had arrived.

That's nice, Mum said vaguely, breaking free of Richard and hunkering down to put a saucepan away.

Mum, it's Bob, I said, quietly.

Bob? Mum said, straightening up. *Your* Bob?

As ever was.

Oh my poor Ashling! Mum said.

Hold on a sec, said Richard. Are you saying that Cindy has got herself involved with Ashling's boyfriend?

Ex-boyfriend. I haven't been seeing him for a couple of months or more.

That's a bit awkward for you, Ashling, all the same, isn't it? Richard said.

It's amazing how men can understate situations, but his voice was full of concern. Really he is a very sweet man.

I don't mind, I said firmly. I really don't mind.

But I did mind. I minded fiercely. I can see that now. At the time, I was trying desperately to salvage some dignity out of the situation, but I minded all right. Though I have no right to mind, I know I haven't. Why did it have to be the noxious Cindy, of all people? I promised myself I wouldn't call her that any more, but sometimes it's hard to be fair.

Wait a minute, said Richard. Is this some horrible form of revenge or something? Is he doing it to spite you? Because if he is, he's behaving like a complete rat, both to you and to Cindy, and I will go right up there and rearrange his face for him so his dentist won't be able to recognise him.

Grrr! said Mum, and bared her teeth at Richard to show she thought he was brave and masterful.

I didn't think it was funny, though. Oh my god! I said, plonking into a chair at the damp kitchen table and kneading my forehead with my knuckles, trying to think. My mind was racing, going over the phone call business again, but this possibility hadn't dawned on me.

He didn't know, Alva said then. I opened the door to him, and he nearly fell over. He definitely didn't know. And anyway, he wouldn't do that. He's very nice, Richard, really nice.

Yes, said Mum. He is. He's a nice lad.

That's right, I said. It's just happened, that's all. But the thing is, what are we going to do now? Keep out of his way, or what?

No, said Richard. We can't cower out here all afternoon. That would be ridiculous. I think you have two options, Ashling. We can all go up to the drawing room now, just as we would do after lunch on any Sunday, and you can say, Oh hi Bob, what a coincidence! and embarrass the hell out of him and take the wind out of Cindy's sails, or we can go up there and let Cindy introduce him to us.

And not let on we *know* him? I asked incredulously.

Yep, said Richard. But you don't have to. It's up to you.

But why? I asked him. Why would I want to do that?

Well, Richard said, this is Cindy's first boyfriend, as far as I know, and I think it would be ... well, I–

It would be spoilt for her if she knew he was one of my cast-offs, I said, finishing his sentence for him.

You put it very crudely, Ashling, Richard said. But yes, that is about the situation. Look, I know she'll probably find out eventually, but just for now, it would be nice for her not to have to face that. That's all.

OK, then, I said, with a sudden spurt of generosity. Let's do it so, Operation Save Cindy's Face!

Yahoo! Alva whooped, and did a little flamenco step, waving Cindy's boot like a castenet. Let's go.

Are you sure, Ashling? Mum asked anxiously.

Yes, I'm sure, I said, but I was talking very fast because I didn't want to stop and think and change my mind. Cindy is not my favourite person, and it wasn't easy being generous to her, especially not after what I'd seen in the hall. When I think about it, I think I was doing it more for Richard than for Cindy. I like him.

I don't want to spoil this for Cindy, I gabbled. It's not her fault. You go first, Richard. Take up some tea or something. Let her introduce him to you first. Then say something like, Cindy must introduce you to the rest of the family, to give him a bit of warning that we're coming in. Try to sound reassuring. He's sure to be on tenterhooks. Then we'll just come and join you, and we won't let on we know him. If everybody just acts natural, it should all go off OK.

What about Bob, though? asked Alva. How's he going to know what we're up to?

Just leave Bob to me, said Mum. As long as this is what Ashling wants.

I think they were all beginning to enjoy the situation. Alva certainly was. She was dancing with excitement now, rather than agitation.

Richard got a teatray together and went off up to the sitting room. We gave him a head start, and then the three of us trooped up together after him.

Cindy was draped along the sofa, with a rug on her knees, looking like the cat that got the cream, and Richard was pouring tea for Bob, who was in an armchair. When we opened the door, Richard said, loudly, Oh, here comes my wife now, and the girls.

It gave me a little shiver to hear him say 'my wife' like that. At least he didn't say we were his daughters. Bob went three shades of red when he saw us at the door and looked as if he was about to say something, but Mum took charge. She locked his eyes with hers, sailed across the carpet, leaving me and Alva still standing in the open doorway, and put out her hand to shake Bob's: Very pleased to meet you, she said, um, eh?

Robbie, Cindy said proudly. His name's Robbie.

That's what his other friends called him. I'd almost forgotten that it was I who'd christened him Bob, and that everyone outside our family calls him Robbie, except his mother, who calls him Robert.

Bob stared at Mum, the colour beginning to drain slowly from his face. She thrust her hand more firmly in the direction of his chest, and eventually he got the message and delivered a limp hand into hers. You could almost hear him swallow with relief.

Oh! said Mum gaily, half to Cindy, half to Bob, I see, Robbie, as in Robert?

Bob said: Oh, um, yes, as in Robert. Only my mother actually calls me Robert though. I get called all sorts of things, Rob, Robbie, Bob, Bobby.

Martin, Cindy added archly, but half under her breath, thinking nobody would get the joke except Bob.

I spluttered at that and had to feign a nose blow to cover it up. I turned around then and shut the door behind me.

And how *is* your mother? Mum was saying, forgetting for a moment that she wasn't supposed to know him.

I could hear Alva beside me drawing her breath in at that, but Cindy didn't seem to notice.

Oh, very well, thank you, Bob answered, very well.

These are my daughters, Ashling and Alva, Mum said smoothly then, turning towards us and we nodded at him and he nodded back. I stumbled from the door and found myself a small, insignificant and very uncomfortable armchair as far away as possible from the family group they were all making in the centre of the room. I began to wish I hadn't agreed to this.

Alva, naturally enough, had no such inhibitions about joining in the little charade. She pranced into the middle of the room, making a dramatic gesture of handing Cindy back her boot. Eventually she plonked herself down on the pouffe at Bob's feet and started to help Richard with the tea. She kept offering things to Bob, biscuits and sugar and milk, with a sly little grin on her face. Bob kept waving her away, afraid to meet her eyes, I think.

I felt very wobbly all through it, so I just sat there on my uncomfortable little chair and didn't say very much. Nobody thought of offering me tea, and I didn't want to draw attention to myself by asking for some or pouring some for myself. All the time I could just see the image of Cindy and Bob in each other's arms in the hall floating in front of me. But the others had this really normal-seeming conversation about nothing at all, making jam, I think it was. I was glad to see Bob go. I never felt like that before.

Cindy asked us afterwards if we had liked him, and Alva said: He's absolutely gorgeous, Cindy, where did you find him?

Cindy tossed her head and said, Oh, just around, you know, but you could see she was delighted. I couldn't very well hate her for liking Bob, now, could I? In fact, watching her gloating over him made me feel a sort of a funny tenderness for her. I was tempted to tell her then, just so we could smile together about him, and tell each other what a nice guy he is, but that would have been a bit pointless at that stage, and anyway, I figured she might turn nasty if she felt we'd made a fool of her.

Ashling never had such a good-looking boyfriend, did you, Ashling? Alva went on slyly, and you could see Cindy preening herself. I choked at that, and Richard had to slap me on the back.

I still wish it was me he called to see today, not Cindy. Life's a bitch, and then you die, as Alva says. And the worst part is that I have only myself to blame.

Thursday 27th November

Things had been getting a bit better around here lately, or so I thought. I thought we were all learning to live with each other, not necessarily to like each other, but at least to tolerate each other. After the Bob episode, I felt I had something in common with Cindy, and I felt, I suppose, that she owed me one, for how I protected her interests that day. Though of course she doesn't owe me anything, especially since she doesn't even know. Sometimes I think maybe that was a bit of a wasted sacrifice as long as Cindy doesn't know I made it.

But then the whole thing blew apart this morning. There was a massive row at breakfast, just because Alva had borrowed Cindy's boots, without asking her. Of course, Alva shouldn't have done it, but I suppose we're used to her doing that sort of thing. We don't take much notice. You couldn't blame Cindy for being annoyed, and I keep trying to remember that this is her home we've all muscled in on, but it is hard to keep seeing it that way when she behaves the way she did this morning. She didn't just get annoyed. She completely over-reacted. She blew her top and really went for Alva. It was awful, just awful. She was like a wild cat. Her eyes flashed with anger and she screamed at her. I didn't know how to make her stop, and I couldn't bear the noise, so in the end I leant over and pulled her hair. This isn't a bit like me, but I was furious with her, absolutely furious, especially after all the allowances I have been making for her lately, after I had started even to like her slightly. It's always three steps forward, two steps back, I suppose, in situations like this, but I'm getting a bit tired of it.

Anyway, this house was not a pleasant place to be this morning. Alva was shaking all the way to school after the row, and I thought Mum was going to have a miscarriage. I rang her school from our school at break, to make sure she was all right. She had just arrived. She said she was fine, but her voice still sounded a bit shaky.

We all kissed and made up this evening. Well, not exactly kissed, but apologised at least. I know people say it's healthier to fight than to let things fester, but it's hard to see that display of anger this morning as healthy. At least having the fight was a normal sort of a thing to do, though, the sort of thing families do, and I suppose it is better than behaving like strangers to each other, better than behaving as if we were all just waiting for the same bus. It's not what you would call family affection or even casual altruism, but it's better than all looking out of the window rather than talk to each other.

Anyway, this is the only family we've all got now, the five of us, and the baby of course. There's no point in fantasising about the family we would *like* to live in. That's what kept Alva miserable for so long.

We can hardly even count Gavin as family any more, nor Dad – we haven't seen either of them for months. It's funny to think that Cindy is going to be closer kin to us now than Gavin, even though Gavin is actually related to us and Cindy's not.

Sunday 30th November

Cindy and Bob went out together last night. I didn't mind. I truly didn't, this time. I made up my mind not to, and it worked.

I lent her my best jumper, one I got for my birthday. It looked well on her, I must say. It's a pale, pale grey, almost silver, and it looked good with her dark hair. And it made a change from that eternal black she's always in. I felt very noble lending it to her, after everything that's happened, but I think she maybe even recognised the nobility of my gesture. She gave my upper arm a little squeeze when I handed the sweater to her, the closest she can get at the moment to an affectionate gesture. Poor old Cindy! I wouldn't like to be her, really, even if she is going out with my Bob.

Wouldn't it be funny, Alva said, as they left, if Cindy married Bob, and then he'd be your brother-in-law.

It wouldn't be a bit funny, I said, throwing a cushion at her, it would be terrible, absolutely terrible, and don't you go predicting things like that, because the last wedding you predicted actually happened. And there are enough steps and halves around here, without adding in-laws into the pot.

Alva has stopped crying in the night. She hasn't done it once all week. Not even the night of the row. I think she's settling down a bit. We all are. It doesn't mean we're not going to fight, of course, but it's beginning to feel just a bit like a family, just a bit like a home.

I don't think I believe in happily ever after any more, Ashling, Alva said then. Do you?

No, Alva, I don't, I said. I believe in happily, but not in ever after. No, definitely not in ever after.

I suppose happily has to be enough on its own then? Alva said, with a tinge of sadness in her voice, as if she was letting go of an enormously important idea.

Yes, I said, I suppose it has. And I suppose you're lucky to get the happily part at all, never mind the ever after.

I suppose you are, she said.

Alva claims Cindy's been keeping a diary too. Wouldn't you just love to read it? she said. Just to find out what the noxious Cindy thinks of us? No, I said, no, I wouldn't. I'd hate it. I can't imagine anything more depressing.

A happy relief, someone said. Can you believe it? A happy relief! Dad said afterwards they meant a happy *release* from pain and suffering, that that's the sort of thing people say, they don't mean it unkindly, but I don't know. A freudian slip you call that. I don't know why he should be so tolerant anyway. He has no right to be tolerant when people say insensitive, senseless things like that. He should be distraught. He should have been jumping down into the grave, sobbing and tearing his clothes, like Romeo, or do I mean Hamlet? That's what you'd expect of a young widower, robbed prematurely of his bride by the evil shadow of death. But no. Maybe it was a happy relief for *him*.

Urbane is the only word I can think of to describe his manner at the funeral. Urbane. Actually, I just learnt that word last week – it means sort of ultra-smooth. Funny how when you learn a new word, you suddenly start to see it everywhere, and then you find uses for it, and before you know where you are, it feels as if you couldn't have lived without it, that there would have been a gap in your way of thinking if you didn't have it. Anyway, it's the perfect word to describe him, standing there at the door of the church, in his best three-piece business suit and that white shirt and wine tie she gave him for Christmas, and that sick gold pocket watch just glinting on his flat belly, gravely shaking hands with people and making conversation, asking people how their children were doing at school. I ask you! I nearly had to stand on his toe at one point, when it looked as if he was going to get into a conversation about a rugby team. God's teeth!

I drew the blinds down, so people would know it had happened at last, the house was in mourning, we were not to be disturbed.

I'd have put crape on the door knocker if I could have found any, but I don't think they make it any more. I thought about tearing up an old pair of black tights, but then I thought that might be a tad tacky. And what did he do? Went around swishing them all up again, the blinds I mean, their little silky knotted cords like dressing gown sashes swinging merrily against the window panes, saying we needed to let in some light and air, that lowering the blinds was a lot of old-fashioned nonsense, and, worst of all, that she wouldn't have wanted it. He seems to have suddenly discovered all sorts of things she would or wouldn't have wanted. She wouldn't have wanted 'The Lord is my Shepherd', he said – too commonplace. She wouldn't have wanted a big funeral, he said, just a simple service. A simple service! Where does he think he is? The Home Counties of England? We don't have simple services in St Patrick's. I'm sure Fr Egan has never used the word 'service' in his life, unless he's talking about that wretched Toyota of his. We just have the standard funeral mass, with all the latest trimmings – someone from the family has to do a reading, and people have to bring up objects at the offertory that are associated with the dead person – very moving I'm sure. What would she have wanted brought up, I wondered. He couldn't be bothered to choose. In the end I went for a copy of *Ulysses*, to represent her literary side, and then I was kind of stumped. Her other main interest was her house, really, but how do you represent that in a thoughtful and reverent way? You couldn't very well carry up an antimacassar or a teatowel – not that she went in for anything as fussy as antimacassars of course. I thought of a copy of *Interiors*, but then it would look a bit silly beside *Ulysses* – sort of the sublime to the ridiculous, really. So in the end I got a little set of doll's-house furniture from one of those specialist shops for serious collectors,

not a toy shop or anything – Georgian I think it was supposed to be, though which George I don't think it mentioned – and I glued it all down on a nice piece of carpet that was left over from the hall-stairs-and-landing, which we had done last year, and made a sort of a little drawing room out of it, very effective with an Adams-type fireplace and all, very tasteful, but I think some of the aunts thought it was childish. Well, who cares? I'm allowed to be childish. I'm only fifteen, after all, and my mother's dead.

There, I've said it now. My mother is dead. It doesn't sound so bad if you say it sort of casually. Well, actually, no, I haven't got a mother any more. One-parent family and all that. She's dead, as a matter of fact. My mother, I mean, you know, dead. As in no longer with us. Safe in the arms of Jesus. Passed away. Gone to her just deserts, I mean, to her reward. Gone to the other side. Gone – just gone, gone, gone, OK? Gone!

Thursday 10th April

God, I hate algebra. Geometry's OK. I like those theorems, sort of a lovely logic to them. But algebra is perverse. (That's my new word for this week. It doesn't mean the same as perverted, *not at all*, I mean, I can be perverse myself sometimes, but I'm not ..., or at least, I don't think I am.) Anyway, if you want perverse, algebra is definitely it. I mean, people deliberately calling numbers X. Do these numbers have a private life they want to keep hidden, I ask myself, or how come they have to have their identities shielded like that? X! It's not even original. Why couldn't they be T or L or something, just for variety? But no, it's always our old friends X and Y.

Sometimes, when I get really bored with algebra, I manage to stage a little diversion. You know, a bit of a fainting fit or something

like that. I read in one of those old school stories of Imelda's (she's my aunt, dead cool, my godmother too, actually) – Mallory Towers, I think the place was called – that you put blotting paper in your shoes. I worried for a while that one of these enthusiastic first aid types might take my shoes off, and my scheme would be exposed, so I had the bright idea of putting the blotting paper in my socks instead. I tried tissues one day, but that didn't work. Seems it has to be good old-fashioned blotting paper. So I tried that. Also I held my breath and thought about injections. That seemed to work. I can't be sure it was the blotting paper, of course, but it probably helped.

But the thing is, now I don't actually have to faint. I just have to get a bit pale or have pinkish eyes and maybe let a discreet little sob escape, and Mr Garvey is throwing windows open and patting me on the back at a great rate. I don't like him patting me on the back like that. He's a bit of a scumbag really. Short men are always trying to over-compensate, to show how sexy they are. I read that in *Seventeen*. Anyway, Mr Garvey – Mr Gravy we call him – is definitely in that category. He's dead hairy. It's kind of gross really, this short skinny little fellow with really white skin, all crawling with thick black hairs. Gives me goosepimples just thinking about him. And I definitely didn't take to having him slapping me on the back. I wonder if I could get him for sexual harrassment? (That's just a joke, by the way.)

Anyway, ever since I fainted two weeks in a row in algebra, and then with him seeing me sobbing my heart out in the cloakroom my first day back after the funeral, I have him where I want him. Or at least I thought I had. I thought I was in control of the situation – until yesterday.

Yesterday, when I bent my head over my book and gave a

pitiful little shudder, like I was trying to suppress my grief, he came right down the centre aisle between the desks and he sat down on the seat beside me – Lisa was out sick that day, monthlies I think, though she seems to have them twice a month, it can happen, you know, especially at our age, something to do with too many hormones – anyway, he sat down beside me and he said, Cindy, I think you should go and see the guidance counsellor, and his knobbly adam's apple sort of wobbled pathetically in his scrawny little neck.

Yeah, my name's Cindy. Naff, isn't it. Like I'm called after a doll or something. My mum's idea. Apparently she wanted to spell it Cyndi, but my dad put his foot down at that. Mum could be a real nerd, sometimes, actually. Give him his due, Dad has a certain sense of decorum. I know it's partly because she was American, and they have what Dad calls 'different cultural values'. He can be so condescending, you wouldn't believe it. Reminds me of someone who hates blacks or travellers, but is trying to make it sound politically correct, though in this case it's Americans he hates, which is politically correct anyway, practically obligatory actually.

Not me. I mean, I call travellers 'tinkers' just to annoy old Iron Knickers McCormack, our RE teacher. She gets on our nerves. Always wanting us to create living liturgies. I'm not entirely sure what that is, but it involves taking your shoes off. You can imagine the pong with twenty-five fifteen-year-olds prancing about in their stockinged feet while old Iron Knickers plays 'Lord of the Dance' on the harmonica.

Anyway, where was I? Oh yes, the guidance counsellor. I told Mr Gravy that I thought the guidance counsellor was for careers. He said yes, but also for personal stuff. I asked him did he think

I had a personal problem, and he said he thought I needed bereavement counselling. You know, the funny thing was, when he said the word 'bereavement' I got all choked up, for real, like, this time. I mean I'd been putting it on before, just to waste a bit of algebra time, but when he came out with the word like that, it had such a lonely, abandoned sound, I felt all tearful and I really wanted to put my head on Gravy's tweedy lapel and have a good sob. Luckily I didn't. I have great composure when I put my mind to it.

It ended up with Gravyface saying he would talk to the guid-ance counsellor person on my behalf if I liked, and I said I did like, 'cause I don't really know Milly-Molly-Mandy. Her real name is Margaret Magee – can you imagine parents who would inflict a name like Margaret on a child whose surname is Magee – I mean, some people have *no* imagination, she was *bound* to be called Maggy-Maggy, and she was for a while, and then we added a third Maggy on for good measure, or rhythm, or something, so then she was Maggy-Maggy-Maggy. I don't exactly know how this got transformed into Milly-Molly-Mandy. Either some wit saw the parallel, or else somebody just made a mistake one day and called her that by accident, and it stuck. (Milly-Molly-Mandy, in case you don't know, is a character in a kids' book, or at least, in lots of kids' books. She is unbearably sweet and good, so you see it's especially appropriate, or you will see after a bit.)

It's all set up for next week. I feel it just sort of happened, but maybe it'll be OK. At least I'll get to leave the classroom for the counselling session. Hope it's during algebra.

Wednesday 16th April

I don't know what it is about Dad. He's so, I don't know, together. Urbane. It's as if he was never married. He's picked up the pieces

of his life and he's just sailing on. Or rather, he's behaving as if there weren't any pieces to pick up. As if nothing was even broken. As if Mum never even existed. He never mentions her.

He just gets up in the morning and makes breakfast, like he always used to while she was sick. He has it all worked out. Puts the percolator on first thing. Then he has a shower and gets dressed. He's fast in the mornings, I'll give him that. He has it down to ten minutes, showering and dressing. As soon as I hear the water thrumming on the bottom of the bath I know it's time to get up, and by the time I have heaved myself out of bed he's gone, leaving the bathroom scented and steaming. By the time I'm showered and dressed, he's downstairs again, sipping coffee and reading *The Irish Times*, and my breakfast is waiting for me. Sometimes it's prunes with yoghurt. Sounds too healthy to be tasty, but I love it. Sometimes it's just toast and marmalade. Occasionally it's fried mushrooms or a grilled rasher or even an omelet. But it's never cornflakes, like it used to be when Mum was in charge. Sometimes I get this desperate longing for a plate of cornflakes with brown sugar and hot milk, but no, not with Dad around. He would just consider that too run-of-the-mill altogether. Anyone at all could have cornflakes with hot milk.

Oh I don't know, how come I get carried away describing breakfast, when what I really want to talk about is Dad's behaviour? It's unnatural. He's unnaturally calm about it all. It makes me uneasy. Either he is totally cold-hearted, or he is numbed, still in shock, or, and this seems to me on balance the most likely scenario, he never loved Mum in the first place, was maybe even thinking of leaving her, when she conveniently developed cancer and let him off the hook.

I look at him sometimes over my prunes and yoghurt – it's a

good time to look at him, breakfast, because he is always stuck into the paper at that hour – and I think to myself, this is a man who disliked his wife. This man with his trim moustache and his double-breasted jacket carefully draped over the back of a kitchen chair. This man with a gold signet ring and membership of an expensive golf-club, a secret buyer of *The Great Composers* – I know, I've seen him slipping it into the shopping trolley at the supermarket when he thinks I'm not looking, you'd think it was *Playboy* he's so furtive about it – this is a merry widower, released from the burden of domestic responsibility and a clinging, houseproud, under-achieving wife.

Yes, I have to admit it. Mum was all those things. She got married young, gave up work almost as soon as she got pregnant, and never looked back. After that, once I was at school, it was all cake sales and coffee-mornings. Then she graduated to book clubs and writers' workshops, and then it was bridge parties and meeting friends for lunch in town, even the occasional cocktail party or exhibition, and endless charity dinners. Last year she joined a wine-tasting group and took up French for about the third time. She took a course in interior design once. She was going to become a consultant, but she never sat the exam. Then she did one of those courses that teaches you how to advise people what colours they should wear. It's all a load of mumbo-jumbo. Either a colour suits you or it doesn't. All this talk about personality types and skin tones and seasons and everything is so much codswallop, as far as I'm concerned, but what I found really offensive about it was the way people could get *totally* hung up on this sort of thing, when the world is full of real issues, you know? Don't get me wrong. I'm not one of these unbearable walking social consciences. I'm not against fashion. I love it, actually, but I think you

have to have a sense of style and if you haven't, forget it. All the skin charts in the world are about as useful as having your horoscope cast when it comes to putting a look together. If you need a system, then it isn't a look.

I like that. If you need a system, then it isn't a look. It might be good for an advertising campaign some time, when I get a job in Creative. I love the sound of that. I'm in the Creative department, actually. Except I'll have to work on pronouncing 'I'm'. You have to say it the way Sinéad O'Connor does. It has to sound like a cross between 'Oi'm' and 'Aahm', not easy.

Thursday 17th April

Well, of course it wasn't during algebra, the counselling session, I mean. That'd be too good to be true. It was during English, which is a shame, because Mr O'Donnell who teaches that is gorgeous and we all have this massive collective crush on him and we have this competition going. Every time he asks a question we all put our hands up, and wave them like mad, whether or not we know the answer. The idea is to get him to ask you. If he does ask you, you've won. Doesn't matter if you don't know – you can just say any old thing. The point is to get him to look at you long enough and to say your name. Bliss, to hear him say your name. I could swoon! He must think we're all terribly enthusiastic. He only has to lift his voice up at the end of a sentence and we're all away, seizing the opportunity of a question and waving our hands like billyo. The poor man is faced with a sea of hands practically every time he looks up from *Julius Caesar*. I answered him once, and whatever I said, I can't remember what it was now, it must have been a bit rude, but anyway, the poor man blushed. He doesn't ask me any more, but I still take part in the competition,

11

for the fun of it. It's gas to see the way he tries not to make eye-contact with me. He knows that if he did, my eyes would burn into his and he'd be forced, against his better judgement, to ask me.

But to get back to Milly-Molly-Mandy and the counselling, it was desperate. I had to sit there and listen to her giving me all this guff about my tender years – I kid you not, she actually used that putrid term – and the importance of a mother figure for a girl of my age, and how I should learn to grieve properly and all this old rubbish. I mean, I know all that stuff. You can read it in *Cosmo* any day. And I did cry and all. I like a good cry, actually. It's my dad who isn't grieving properly I told her, and she got all interested and wanted to know about my relationship with my father. Well, I just stared. Relationship! What a word! He's just my father, I said. You'd think he was a fella, the way she was talking. Also, she has this unnerving habit when she is talking of stopping in the middle of a sentence, in the middle of a word even, and sort of sucking in a breath between her teeth and swallowing a whole lot of saliva, quite audibly. Then she lets out a long moist sort of sigh before she continues. I don't know whether she has some sort of a plumbing problem in her mouth, or whether she just does it for effect. Effect, I think. It makes the other person very nervous, because you are left waiting for the next word in the sentence and she has to do her oral flushing bit first. Maybe she does it to make sure you are listening, hanging on her words.

Anyway, she got all serious then and started on about somebody called Electra in Ancient Greece. She fell in love with her father, apparently. I mean, give me a break. He's not the most delightful person in the world, my dad. In fact, he is positively objectionable. But he's not, *you* know, well he just isn't. I suppose I'm lucky

really. What some kids have to put up with is not funny. Still, losing your mother when you are only fifteen does not exactly make you the apple of Lady Luck's eye, so I suppose I shouldn't get too carried away about how great my life is.

The upshot of it all was, anyway, that Milly-Molly-Mandy wants to meet Dad. I told her I didn't think he'd appreciate her trying to counsel him, but she said she wouldn't dream of it, she just wanted to talk to him about me. I don't see the point. I mean, I told her he's the one that needs counselling. No good will come of this, mark my words.

Monday 21st April

Dad's come out. About *The Great Composers*, I mean. He must have twigged that you can hide a stack of magazines in your bedroom, but it's difficult to hide a collection of CDs, and there is not much point in acquiring the best hundred tunes in the world or whatever it is supposed to be if you can't play any of them. So now it's official. We are a family that gets *The Great Composers* – how low can you sink? – and the house is full of 'Eine Kleine Nachtmusik' and the march from *Aida* and Ravel's 'Bolero' and 'The Four Seasons' from morning till night. It's OK, especially the bit from *Aida*. I saw that on the telly once, and it's kind of cool, especially at the end, where this fabulously beautiful black woman – I bet she's never even heard of Colour Me Beautiful, but she is all style – goes off into a tomb with her lover and they die a terrible death, buried alive for love. Mad!

Anyway, there I was trying to learn my history homework and listening to one of Dad's Great Composers, Palestrina I think it was – have you ever heard of Palestrina? sounds like a flavour of ice cream, doesn't it, or a make of sports car – when the phone

rang. Let him answer it, I thought. I was comfy on the sofa, with a rug pulled up to my chin. But it rang and rang. Dad must be in the garden, or in the loo or somewhere, I thought, so eventually I answered it. Old Milly-Molly-Mandy. For a split second I was tempted to say, Wrong number, and hang up and then quickly take the phone off the hook, but I figured I would only be staving off the evil day, so I went and got my runners on and waded out through the weedbed that passes for a lawn in our house and found Dad clearing out the old shed at the bottom of the garden. I gabbled something to him about bereavement counselling and janey mac if he didn't burst into tears, right there in front of me, leaning on a spade. I didn't know where to look. At least he's human, I thought. Funny how the word 'bereavement' seemed to do it. It had nearly the same effect on me. I stood there for a moment and considered whether I should fall weeping on his neck and have a touching scene, widowed father and orphaned daughter console each other sort of thing, but then I thought, hey, no, he wasn't there for you when you had the weepies, remember? But I wasn't actively cruel. I gave him a few manly thumps on the back, and said, There, there, come on now. Are you going to talk to old Milly-Molly-Mandy or not?

He took his hanky out – he always has one, and it's always cotton, pure affectation – and blew his nose a few times, dreadful sound, like an elephant with sinus trouble, and pulled himself together.

He was ages on the phone. Old Palestrina had played himself out, and I'd got through half of Rachmaninov before he came in. He was still pretty mucky from the garden, so he didn't sit down, just held onto the doorknob and said that he'd had a long chat with Ms Magee (I ask you, does anyone else in the world actually

pronounce Ms?) and had agreed to go and see her. Good luck to him, I thought.

Wednesday 30th April

He wouldn't tell me how he got on with Milly-Molly-Mandy last week, but yesterday evening, there I was doing my homework, with The Simpsons turned down really low, when he announced, cool as a breeze, that dinner was ready, and would I hurry please, that he had to go out. He was in such a rush he didn't even notice the TV was on, which is strictly against the rules while I'm doing my homework. It is a pretty stupid rule actually, because it helps me to think. I can't stand all the silence in this damned house.

I winkled it out of him over the spaghetti bolognese. Off for another meeting with Milly-Molly-Mandy if you don't mind. What can they possibly have to talk about? I mean, it can't be me still. I'm OK. Maybe she ignored my advice about Dad and is trying to sort him out herself. These amateur psychologists. They think they know it all. Well, it's her funeral. Oops! Didn't mean that. Her lookout, then. She's welcome to him.

Thursday 1st May

He didn't get home until all hours last night. Well it was only half-past eleven but that *is* all hours on a weeknight. I'm at that awkward age, too old for a babysitter, too young to leave on my own after midnight, or so he says, and to be perfectly honest sitting around at the witching hour with only the late-night movie for company is not exactly my idea of a cool way to spend an evening. I rang Lisa after I'd finished my homework and had washed up – yes, I do wash up, every second evening, we take it in turn, very

democratic. Anyway, Lisa hadn't even got halfway through her homework, so she couldn't stay on the phone for a natter. Funny how parents have this idea that teenagers spend all their time on the phone locked into eternal meaningless conversations. It's not true. Just another stereotype. Another manifestation of the generation gap. (That's Dad's word. He has all these phrases from the seventies.)

Give him his due, he never leaves me on my own late at night, so even half-eleven was late for him. And considering that he left the house at seven, that was a long chat he must have been having with her ladyship. Not that I care. Couldn't give a fiddler's, just so long as I can be sure it's not me they're talking about. But I don't think so. At least, I hope not.

Monday 5th May

This is getting to be ridiculous. Yesterday lunchtime the phone rang. We had just got back from mass. Yes, we do go, though I know for a fact Dad doesn't believe in anything, with the possible exception of the report of the closing prices on the Stock Exchange. We had gone to the grave afterwards, so that's why it was lunchtime when we got home. I hate going to the grave. It's all so raw still, all earth and stuff, the grass hasn't really settled in again properly yet. It's one of those grassy cemeteries, which is quite nice, just rows of headstones and lots of grass. Sort of open plan death, you could call it. No actual little marble walls around the graves and absolutely none of those awful pointy stone chips. But of course our grave doesn't have a headstone yet. They explained to me why you don't put a headstone on a new grave, and believe me, you do not want to know. So there's just this makeshift sort of wooden cross thing, stuck into the earth at a rakish angle. It's

all too, oh I don't know, too real or something, and I just get depressed there, thinking of her with all that earth weighing her down, which you wouldn't think if the grave was all smooth and grassy and part of the general rolling lawn effect.

Anyway, we had just got in, with a stick of French bread and two chocolate croissants from the French bakery – bakeries in our area are open on Sundays now, very continental, don't you know – and the *Sunday Tribune*, and there was this absolutely delicious smell of roasting lamb and rosemary and garlic, because this was one of the Sundays where we go in for the traditional Sunday lunch. Some Sundays we do that, we make it a proper Sunday and do the whole bit, the graveyard and the French bakery and the roast, but other Sundays we just stay in bed and listen to 'Sunday Miscellany'. At least, I do. I don't know what he listens to. Probably exactly the same. Except *he* probably thinks *I'm* listening to Atlantic or Rock 104 or something, which shows how much he knows about me.

So there we are, sniffing the air and looking forward to our lunch and a lazy afternoon reading the paper – at least I was planning to go over to Lisa's after lunch and maybe go somewhere, into town, for a milkshake in Eddie's Diner or something like that – when the phone starts shrieking at us, before we'd even got our coats off. We're still wearing coats, even though it's May. Dad pushed past me. I swear, he nearly knocked me over in his eagerness to get to the phone first. He picks it up and he's all smiles, even before he hears who it is. He knew who it was. He had to have known. Otherwise, why would he have been grinning like an idiot before she even spoke? He'd been expecting her call. It was a prearranged thing.

I sat on the bottom step of the stairs while he was talking to

17

her, pretending to read the newspaper. It was all the usual stuff, not very interesting really, and far too much sports coverage, but I sat there grimly for a good ten minutes while he muttered into the phone.

He ignored me when he hung up, just walked past me into the kitchen and started fussing with oven gloves. I don't get it. What's the big deal here? He couldn't possibly fancy her, could he? I mean, she's not even pretty. She has blondish hair, cut like a bush, exactly like a work of topiary, actually, all sticking out from her head so that from the back – she's very slender, I'll give her that – she looks for all the world like a small bay tree, the sort they have in tubs outside Italian restaurants. I suppose she is not actually unattractive. She has a nice smile. But what a name! And what a job!

I told Lisa the whole story today. I didn't meet her after all yesterday. I was too busy trying to think this business through, so I just hung around the house for the afternoon, tidied my room, got out the handful of T-shirts and single cotton skirt that constitute my entire summer wardrobe in case we have a summer, cooked the tea – always sausages on a Sunday – and then had a bath and washed my hair, cut my toenails, pampered myself with creams and unguents, and went to bed early with a book and half a bar of Bourneville.

Lisa hooted with laughter when I told her, and I had to make her swear she wouldn't breathe a word about this to anyone. I could see she was dying to blurt it all over the school. So I told her I was very upset at the idea of my Dad having a girlfriend so soon after my mother's death, and I managed to muster up a tear or two, so that shut her up, and she promised she wouldn't breathe a word to a living soul. I gave a convincing little wince at that

expression, and embarrassed her no end, so that should keep her quiet. Anyway, the point is, Lisa agrees. She thinks they must be 'seeing each other'. It can't all be bereavement counselling, not if she's ringing him up on a Sunday lunchtime.

Friday 9th May

Lisa has been doing a bit of snooping on old Milly-Molly-Mandy, or the Bay Tree, as I now call her. Lisa fell about when I told her that. Well, at least she did after I explained what a bay tree was. It turns out she's a single parent – the Bay Tree that is, not Lisa, obviously. Except she used to be married, so it doesn't count, or not in the same way as being an unmarried mother anyway. Still, she's not a widow, which is the only truly respectable way you can be a single parent. She has two daughters, one a year older than me, one a year younger. I must ask Lisa where she got all this lovely information. I was so interested in what she found out that I forgot to ask her how she did it.

It turns out that Magee is her married name, so I take back all that stuff about her parents giving her such an impossible name, but I do think she might have thought about the consequences when she married Mr Magee, whoever he was, and kept her own name, for aesthetic reasons if not from feminist principles. Though mind you, she might have been called something awful to start with, like Hogg.

The daughters go to a mixed school, one of those Protestant places where you have to pay fees and play hockey. Maybe their father is a Protestant, though I don't think Magee is a very Protestant name. A Protestant father would be quite exotic, and it could explain why they are divorced or separated or whatever the word is. Catholics aren't allowed to. Well, they do, but they

19

aren't supposed to, so it might be easier if you were a Prod, I suppose. But what I want to know is why they broke up – apart from his being a Protestant, I mean. There has to be a reason. I wonder does she make a habit of falling for other men, like my father? Maybe she has a history of it. Maybe she kept doing it while they were married, and he just got fed up and left her. Probably that's what happened. I mean, you couldn't blame him, really, could you?

Monday 12th May

Dad's given up weeping over his garden spade and grinning idiotically into the telephone receiver, so that's something to be grateful for. I think maybe the little fling with Mrs Magee must be over, because the telephone hasn't been for him once all week, and he stayed in every night except one, when he had to meet a business associate. That's a relief. I really didn't like the direction that was going in.

The phone hardly rings at all these days. Imelda rang me a few days ago, Just keeping in touch, petal – that's what she calls me – and then she asked to speak to him, but that was just out of politeness, I know it was really me she wanted to talk to. And then there were a few phone calls for the hotel in the next road, whose phone number is almost identical to ours. Windsor Court or Hampton House or something it's called, something English anyway. Funny how people get cross when you tell them it's a wrong number – even though they're the ones who've made the mistake. Makes me mad that, I feel like screaming obscenities into the mouthpiece at them, but I don't. I can be very self-disciplined at times. But that's about all. If it wasn't for the occasional phone call from Lisa, who is eternally forgetting her

homework notebook and needs to check out what we have to do, I'd nearly think people were avoiding us.

Anyway, after the fuss about the Bay Tree died down, Dad went a bit funny, as I say, and started getting all fatherly and concerned about me. Yesterday, he suggested we go 'out for a drive'. Now, if there is one thing I cannot abide it is going 'out for a drive'. It seems so pointless to me, getting into the car and just going anywhere, any old place. The way I look at it, a car is just a mode of transport, something for taking you places you want to go. Going just 'out for a drive' seems to me a distortion of the whole point of a car, not to mention the waste of petrol and the damage to the environment. I told him all this, as I was buckling my seatbelt, and he put on that long-suffering look he does so well and said that actually he had been going to propose we go down the dual carriageway and have an early lunch at a little restaurant he knows in Kilmacanogue with a nice garden and outside tables. Well, that cheered me up. I know the place he means, and it is very pleasant, as Mum used to say. She had these little pat phrases she used to use. That was one of them: 'a very pleasant lunch', 'a very pleasant evening'. I think she used to collect non-American phrases and practise them, and then she would forget that they were a sort of language-learning exercise and instead of assimilating them into her normal vocabulary she would get particularly attached to them and overuse them. It was one of those things Dad and I used to scoff at her about. We went in for scoffing at Mum a bit, I have to admit, but it was all in fun. I miss her.

Anyway, there we were having this lovely broccoli soup they do there with brown scones, delicious and good for you too, which is an unusual enough combination, and gazing at the trees, all

feathery with new leaves and sort of fresh-washed looking in the sunlight, when he starts asking me how I am. I said I was fine, had a touch of a headache one day last week, but that was only because my glasses were broken and I'd been squinting at the blackboard. No, no, I mean how *are* you, he asked, all earnestly, not waiting for me to explain how I'd had to borrow a few quid from his jeans pocket to pay the optician, which until that moment I had forgotten to tell him about. Then I twigged, he meant how was I psychically, you know, 'in myself'. Oh lord, I thought, this is the Bay Tree talking. Well, I told him I was perfectly all right, which I am. But that didn't seem to satisfy him. He kept going on about 'our loss' and I felt quite uncomfortable. I didn't finish the soup. Then he went on about 'a girl of your age'. Oh no, I thought, don't let him say 'tender years', but of course he did. It was dead embarrassing really. I mean, I was afraid for one awful moment he was going to ask me did I know the facts of life or did I need money for a new bra or anything. He didn't of course, but really it was a moment I would rather forget.

Tuesday 13th May

I've been thinking about our pleasant lunch. I mean, is Dad genuinely trying to get in touch with me, after all these months of aloofness, or what? There's something fishy about this. Was he testing the waters, seeing how I'd react to something that he then decided not to tell me? Or was he genuinely concerned about how I am 'in myself'? This is all very puzzling.

Wednesday 21st May

I'm really disappointed in Dad. It's so sneaky, that's what kills me

about it. There he was that Sunday being all fatherly and concerned, and now this.

The doorbell rang this evening at about half-past five. That'll be the milkman, I thought. Actually it's a girl on a bike. Her dad is the milkman. He does the deliveries in the mornings, and she comes around on Wednesday evenings to collect the money. They make a good team, all neatly worked out, division of labour and all that. I wonder if she has a mother? Anyway, I was just stirring the tomato sauce into the mince – I'm afraid it was the sort of tomato sauce that you get in a jar, Mum would die a thousand deaths, and I have to admit that our diet has come to rely rather heavily on pasta – and I yelled up to Dad, who was upstairs changing out of his office gear, I'll get it, and I pulled the saucepan off the gas and went to get the money out of the cutlery drawer, where we keep cash for everyday expenses like milk and bread and the newspaper. But there wasn't enough, so I went upstairs to ask Dad for some money.

I knocked at his bedroom door, which was closed. I thought that was odd, because he usually leaves it ajar, even when he's changing, even at night he sleeps with it slightly open. Anyway, I knocked, and without waiting for a reply I opened the door and walked in. I mean he was only changing from a jacket into a jumper. He wasn't likely to be starkers or anything, and he wouldn't have passed out with embarrassment even if he'd been stalking around in his socks and underpants. We're not exactly naturists in our house, but we don't go in for major coyness either. Anyway, he was fully dressed, except he wasn't wearing any shoes, and he was sitting on the edge of the bed with the upstairs phone in his hand, chortling away into it. He didn't even hear me, he was so intent.

I stood there with the doorknob in my hand and said loudly and as coldly as I could manage, I need money for the milkman, Dad. He jumped. Then he put his hand over the mouthpiece and hissed, God, don't you ever knock? I didn't bother to answer, because I had knocked, but he'd been so deep in his lovetalk that he hadn't even heard me. I just held out my hand, and he dug into his pocket and handed me a fiver, without looking at me. Before I had even closed the door he was back murmuring down the line, and just as I pulled the door behind me I saw his toes curling and uncurling with pleasure inside his black socks there on the carpet. It was disgusting.

I asked him over dinner why he thought it necessary to make secret phone calls, and he went pink. He tried to wriggle out of it, said he wasn't doing it in secret, he just happened to be in his room when he thought of making the call so he made it up there. I pointed out that he had shut the door. He said he was entitled to shut his own bedroom door, that he was entitled to a bit of privacy in his own house, and that I wasn't to go barging into his room like that again. Tried to turn the whole thing around and make out I was sneaking around watching him, when all I was doing was behaving perfectly normally. I told him I'd knocked, but he didn't believe me, and told me it was time I grew up and stopped treating my parents' room as if it was an extension of my own.

That is just so unfair, but I see it for what it is, a diversionary tactic. Anyway, it's all pretty clear now. Dad is having a secret affair with the Bay Tree. At least, I assume it's the Bay Tree. He must have twigged that I was getting suspicious and so he told her not to ring him at home. I bet that meeting last week with a business associate (I mean, what an expression, I should have

known that nobody says that sort of thing in real life) was really 'a date' with her, as he'd say himself. He's probably 'doing a line' with her. Adults can be so sick sometimes.

Friday 23rd May

It makes you wonder. I mean, Mum is not even two months dead, and there he is throwing himself at another woman. How could he be so callous? He can't have loved her at all. Or maybe he did just at the beginning. I mean, there's me, after all, so there must have been *something* there at one time. I was born six months after they were married. Mum used to joke about it, say I was a miracle baby. When I was small, I used to believe it, that I was really amazingly premature, but when I got older, I realised she was only joking, that she was pregnant when she got married. I used to be proud of that. I felt it proved my parents were unconventional and passionate. Now it makes me wonder. Maybe she pressurised him into marrying her. Maybe she even got pregnant on purpose so he'd have to marry her. Maybe she only wanted an Irish passport. (I haven't worked out why, though, that's still a bit obscure.)

I often wondered why I was an only child. I assumed it was something gynaecological. Mum used to have a terrible time with her periods, and when I was about ten she finally had a hysterectomy, so I thought that was it. But now I wonder. Maybe they had given up sleeping together. I mean, they always had a double bed, but you know what I mean, though now I come to think of it, Dad used to spend a lot of time in the spare room, even before she got sick. Maybe he's been a philanderer all along. The pig.

We've reached a sort of truce, Dad and I. He doesn't ring Margaret, as he now openly calls her, when I am in the house, and she never rings him. But they go out one night a week, and although he doesn't say he is going out with her, at least he doesn't pretend he isn't, if you see what I mean, and he's never late home. I suspect they have lunch together some days too.

Lisa says it's all rather sweet and touching, that it just shows he's a man who needs love in his life. Lisa is interested in love. She is also interested in a lot of other rubbish, such as horoscopes. It's all very well for her. She comes from a nice normal family. She's the eldest of five children and her mother job-shares with another nurse and her grandmother lives across the road and gives them their dinner on her mother's working days and her father coaches football in the local primary school in his spare time and they both always turn up to parent–teacher meetings and one or other of them is always on some committee to do with the residents' association or one of their children's schools. I mean, that's my idea of family life. Going out for a drive with your father and having broccoli soup just doesn't compare. The graveyard and the French bakery on a Sunday aren't really in the same league as what goes on in Lisa's house on a Sunday. Not that I've ever been there, but I can imagine. They probably play Cluedo after lunch or do charades around the fire. I bet they don't get *The Great Composers* either. Lisa's father wouldn't know a Great Composer if one came up and played a quartet in his left ear. But they probably sing rounds when they go places in the car, and I bet their mother buys a copy of *Family Circle* occasionally and makes delicious recipes out of it and they most probably make each other

things out of felt and raffia for Christmas, like the Trapp family.

Oh dear. Christmas. I hadn't thought of that. Well, you don't in June, do you, but I mean, I hadn't thought of Christmas without Mum.

Sunday 8th June

Junior Cert starts tomorrow. English first. That'll be fine. Between my natural flair and Mr Gorgeous O'Donnell I have that all sewn up.

Wednesday 18th June

Finished the exam. It was a doddle really. Mum used to say it was a curse to be bright. I never understood that. I've always found it makes life so much easier if you don't have to kill yourself working and still come out with top grades. I don't think being bright was ever a curse to Mum. Poor Mum. Life was a struggle for her really, all those French lessons and creative writing classes. She must have been floundering like mad. She couldn't even spell, but I suppose that was partly because of being American. She was awfully pretty, though, before she became ill, I mean. How could Dad have treated her like that? The swine.

The others are going on a drinking binge tonight. I couldn't be bothered. I think that sort of thing is terribly immature.

Thursday 19th June

I don't believe it. The very first day after my exams – when every other fifteen-year-old in the country has a hangover – he springs this on me. Said he was waiting till I'd finished to break the news. I was looking forward to just lounging about the house for a bit,

doing a bit of sunbathing in the back garden, getting a few Ruth Rendells out of the library, sipping mint julep (I got the recipe for this out of a colour supplement, but that's neither here nor there, it's still delicious), maybe inviting a few friends over for a barbecue some evening, just not having to think or worry for a change. And then he says he's been planning this 'little holiday' – himself, myself and the three Magees.

This is *not* a *little* holiday, Dad, I pointed out, with icy precision. This is a major life-event. Do you realise, I asked, this is our first holiday without Mum? And you expect me to spend it in the company of three complete strangers? He blenched when I mentioned about our first holiday without Mum. (Blenching is a thing people do a lot in books, but it's not the sort of thing you ever expect to see people do in real life. It's a bit like wringing their hands in that respect. But he blenched all right. It's pretty dramatic, but you'd need to see it to understand. I don't think I could describe it.) He clearly hadn't thought of it that way. Well, he should have. The stupidity of the man is surpassed only by his insensitivity.

He covered up by saying they were not three complete strangers, that I'd known Margaret for three years. I can't imagine how he reached that conclusion. I've been in the school for three years, and she has too, but it is a school of seven hundred girls and, oh, maybe fifty staff. This is not a situation of intimacy, I pointed out. I never spoke to the woman until that bloody counselling session, and I haven't spoken to her since, except on the phone once or twice.

Anyway, the upshot of it was I refused point-blank to go. And no, I don't think that was unreasonable of me. It was unbelievably unreasonable of him to expect me to. He used all sorts of

arguments. That it would be a pretty miserable holiday for both of us if we went together alone. I could see the point of that one, actually. It could be a dreadful strain. It's bad enough just the two of us sharing this house sometimes. But if that really was the point, he could have asked Lisa along, or Imelda. Now there was a good idea. Why couldn't he ask Imelda to come on holiday with us?

I know why. It's not just that he wanted to go with Margaret. It's that Imelda embarrasses the hell out of him. His own sister. I agree she's a bit unusual. For a start, she's a Thalidomide victim, which means she has no proper arms, just sad little hands coming out of her shoulders. She doesn't use her hands much – well, you can't if they're attached directly to your shoulders – and she does most things with her feet, including smoking cigarettes. She's not really a smoker, she only has about one every two or three weeks, but I swear, she saves them up to have in our house, just to shock him. He can't bear it when she lights up. I don't think it's the smoking itself – he's not paranoid about cancer or anything, not even with Mum and all – it's the fact that she does it with her feet. He thinks it's grotesque.

I've known Imelda all my life, so I can't imagine her with arms, but I know it's a bit of a shock for other people when they meet her first. The first time Lisa met her, it was in our house, she was doing something in the kitchen, I don't know, making a sandwich or something like that. Lisa came into the room and saw Imelda struggling with something, and she rushed over all helpfully to her and said, Oh, can I give you a hand? She nearly died of embarrassment when she realised what she'd said. She went bright, bright red. It took Imelda a minute to get it. Then she burst out laughing. She sat down on a chair and she rocked with

laughter. Lisa started to laugh too, but mainly from relief, I think. Anyway, they've been friends ever since.

Friday 20th June

Dad proposed a compromise solution, and I am considering it. It's that he and Margaret can go away together for a long weekend. (It was a long weekend that was in question all along, not a full-length holiday. Even Dad wouldn't be so stupid as to think we could all survive two weeks of each other's company.) I am to spend that weekend with Imelda. I don't know what the Magee girls are supposed to do, but that is their problem. And, this is the compromise bit, we are to have the Magees over for lunch on Sunday week, all three of them, the Sunday before their weekend away.

Saturday 21st June

I agreed to the compromise. I don't see that I have much choice, really. If he invites people to lunch, I have to put up with it. I don't have to be nice to them after all. That wasn't part of the agreement. I didn't actually agree even to be here. I could easily invite myself to Imelda's that day, or I could even wangle an invitation out of Lisa, I'm sure, but I don't think I'll do that. I'm kind of curious actually.

Tuesday 24th June

The more I think about that holiday proposal, the crazier it seems. Could he possibly have done it deliberately to make me accept the lunch invitation without a fight? He's a devious animal, when all's said and done.

I don't know where to begin. The menu, maybe, as that's the simplest part. He did his famous roast lamb with rosemary and garlic, with all the trimmings, mint sauce, redcurrant jelly, roast spuds, glazed parsnips, *petits pois* (frozen of course), and to give him his due it was absolutely delicious. He served a nice Australian Cabernet Sauvignon with it, but that's another story. No starter. He says it's not traditional for Sunday lunch. I think that was quite daring of him, as he was clearly out to impress, but really it showed a certain innate taste. Egg mayonnaise or prawn cocktail would have been just too much. Afterwards we had baked Alaska, which is truly gross, but it's the only dessert he knows how to make that involves the oven – needless to say he didn't dare to enlist my help – and he thought he should do something from the oven since it was on anyway for the lamb. He has this rather endearing little economical streak occasionally.

The younger Magees thought the baked Alaska was scrum, even though it wasn't quite a success – I don't think the oven was hot enough. They are that sort of family. People who use words like 'scrum'. Can you imagine? They wore *kilts*, one in greens and one in blues. They looked like two little girls dressed up to go out to Sunday lunch, which is what they were, except they aren't little. I bet their mother had them in matching clothes when they were smaller. You know, two little tartan dresses from Laura Ashley, and two matching velvet hairbands. They were, as you will have gathered from this description, unspeakable. Oh yes, and they both had little pearl stud ear-rings, just like their mother's. No wonder the father bailed out. Between Miss Prim and Miss Proper and the Bay Tree he must have had a dog's life. I can imagine

what their house must be like. I bet they have swagged curtains and a glass-and-brass coffee table, like a hotel, only in miniature. And back issues of *The Reader's Digest* in the loo. Ashling plays the double-bass, can you imagine anything more lugubrious?

I wore jeans and a HMV sweatshirt, and I alternated between feeling really cool and hip and, well, normal, and feeling sort of coarse and out of place in this frightfully genteel gathering. I have to admit that I drank too much wine. Dad is pretty laid back about alcohol. I think he has this theory that if children drink at home and with parental approval they are less likely to drink because of peer pressure and so to abuse alcohol. I agree with that theory, actually, and I think I am a shining example of its soundness most of the time. Some people at school go to the pub every Friday night and get paralytic. Admittedly, that only takes two pints of lager, but still, I think it's pretty revolting. I have the odd glass of wine on a Sunday with my dad, and that's as far as it goes – usually.

But this Sunday was a bit different. I had my usual glass of wine – Ashling, who is sixteen, was allowed a quarter of a glass, topped up with water, why bother? I thought, it might as well be Ribena at that dilution – and then I snuck another glass, more out of boredom really than anything else. After that, I just kept pouring. Nobody noticed. Well, precisely. I might as well not have been there, as far as the lovebirds were concerned, and as for Little Miss Moffat and Miss Goody-Two-Shoes, they were too busy wiping their mouths carefully with their napkins and saying please and thank you and would you ever pass the butter. They said nothing else throughout the whole meal, just chewed with great concentration.

I felt thoroughly left out. I realised afterwards why. The others were in pairs. The courting couple and the sisters. Only muggins

was on her own, sticking out like a sore thumb. I'm beginning to understand why dinner parties are usually arranged to be in even numbers. There is a lot to be said for conventional etiquette, in moderation of course. Now, the pair sitting opposite me – they took one side of the dining table, and Dad and Margaret sat at either end, with me on my lonesome on the other side – for all they looked like a picture out of a Marks and Spencer catalogue, they hadn't a clue really how to behave. Please and thank you and using your napkin are all very well, but true courtesy involves making the other person feel less uncomfortable. They don't know the first thing about true courtesy.

So I just sipped away quietly at the Cabernet Sauvignon, and after a bit a sort of a rosy glow descended and I stopped caring about being the only unpartnered person in the room. I probably talked a bit much. I usually do, after a glass of wine, but I don't think I said anything shameful. I certainly felt rather warm about the cheeks, and I may have been a bit on the waspish side about the baked Alaska. I can't be sure. But I know I didn't do or say anything truly outrageous. I know that at one point I told Margaret all the teachers' nicknames. She didn't understand most of them, including her own.

I fell asleep afterwards. We all went into the drawing room (Mum's word – in her attempt to be unAmerican, like most foreigners she often erred on the side of being too English) after lunch for coffee, and this was the point where I fell asleep. I'm sure they all had a great giggle about it, but ignorance is bliss to a blind horse, or whatever.

They woke me up after a while, and made me put on a jacket and go for a walk on Dún Laoghaire pier. Dún Laoghaire pier is a lovely place: bracing air, pretty view, the fine misty spray of the

ocean and all that. But there is nothing more excruciating than walking along it on a Sunday afternoon with two girls in kilts after just a drop too much wine. I swear to God, they actually linked me, one on either side. Not heartily or anything. Just like old ladies on an afternoon out from their nursing home. They didn't say a word, just linked me along the pier, under the bandstand bit and right down to the lighthouse place and then a quick spin and back again to the icecream van at the other end, and Dad and Margaret linked each other too and toddled along ahead of us. What has my life come to, that I should spend a Sunday afternoon like this?

Wednesday 2nd July

I went into town yesterday and bought a long black T-shirt and a pair of black leggings. I think I am still in shock after the kilts, and this is my way of coping with it, going to the opposite extreme. I never went in much for fads like all black gear, but now I'm beginning to see the point. It is a statement of dissent from velvet hairbands. I told Dad this when he asked. He hadn't a clue what I meant, of course. He said I looked as if I was in mourning. Really? I said as caustically as I could manage and he had the grace to blush. The only problem is that I only have my runners and my brown school shoes. I'll have to save up for suitable footwear. My resources have all been used up on the clothes.

Thursday 3rd July

I can hardly believe it. As he was leaving for work this morning — I get up early, even though it's the hols, as I don't like to think of him eating his prunes on his own, I feel I owe him that much, he

makes such a ritual of mornings – he threw me thirty quid and said, I don't think I can bear those brown shoes with the black gear. Get yourself some black shoes. I was stunned. Thirty quid is in the birthday present league.

Friday 4th July

High as a flag on the... Well, not exactly. I got a pair of Docs with the thirty quid. They look great, but they're a bit heavy for July. Still, I like the look. Dad sighed when he saw them, but he didn't comment. He can't afford to say anything, can he, off on his dirty weekend this evening.

Sunday 6th July

Imelda is a pet. She went out of her way to make sure I had a good time this weekend. It's not her fault if I'm miserable. Friday night I spent at Lisa's, and then on Saturday, I went window-shopping in town with Lisa – neither of us had any money – and then we went to the Green. We had to wade through a huge gaggle of Spaniards that had gathered swarming outside Habitat and were making a horrendous gobbling noise, like a thousand turkeys who've just heard about Christmas. We managed to avoid being sucked in and chewed and spat out by them, just about by the skin of our teeth, and ran away across the road to the sanity of the duckpond, where we sat and watched children feeding the ducks.

It must be nice to be that little. Mum used to take me, I remember, when I was very young, on the bus, and we'd bring a paper bag full of stale bread. I'm sure it's terribly bad for them, but they seem to love it. I wonder if ducks get heart attacks. Lisa says that's a loadarubbish (one of her favourite expressions at the

35

moment). Lisa can be just a little unsympathetic at times.

She had to go off then to cook the children's tea. Her mother takes Saturdays off from family responsibilities and Lisa and her dad divide the day into shifts between them. It sounds such a cosy arrangement, but Lisa says it's a drag. I suppose it might be, if you really had to do it.

When Lisa went home, I wandered along to Imelda's place. It's a flat near the canal, an apartment I should say. She has all these cool gadgets that she had put in by the builders when they were building the apartment. She has these really sensitive taps. They nearly turn on if you so much as look at them. And she got them to do it all open plan, because, as she says, it is ridiculous to slice up a space of this size into conventional rooms that are too small to swing a cat, even too small for a Thalidomide person to swing a Manx cat (her joke, not mine, so it's not in bad taste).

Her place looks like something out of an American TV programme, you know the sort, where the kitchen is in one corner, on a sort of a little stage, and you can see the front door from the fridge, except she has an ordinary doorbell that goes bzzz instead of the ones that go ding-dong, like they have on those shows. (I have never been to America, despite being half-American, so my impressions of that country are entirely based on TV. My mother was adopted or fostered or something, and she doesn't have a proper family, so it's not like there are grandparents to go and see or anything.)

And she has a mezzanine bedroom, which means it's not a proper room, just a sort of floating platform above the main room. You'd think she would find it difficult to get up the steep little staircase to reach it, but she manages. It's great, except that there is a bit of a problem if you have fried onions. You can't get away

from the smell. So don't eat fried onions, she says with a shrug (onion slicing is not exactly her favourite thing to do anyway, I imagine), but unfortunately it applies to a few other things as well, such as Indian takeaway, which is what we had on Saturday.

I washed up afterwards. That is a golden rule you learn in an open-plan flat. Never leave the dishes until tomorrow. Then we went to the cinema and we missed the last bus because the movie was over late and we went for coffee afterwards in Bewley's anyway, so we walked home. It's only about a mile. It was a lovely balmy summer's evening, and we sauntered along the canal. Well, actually, my new boots were hurting a bit, so sauntered is a bit of an exaggeration. Imelda sauntered. She was wearing an ankle-length dress and she looked very graceful, which sounds silly about someone who has no arms but really she did. I had thrown a smart jacket over her shoulders, and you'd never guess really. The moon was like a big bright coin in the sky and it was reflected in the stilly depths of the canal. We stopped to admire it – the reflection I mean, which was somehow more eerie, more lunar even, than the moon itself, which is of course anyway really only a reflection, or at least its light is. Then she said, Those boots are killing you, Cindy. Take them off, why don't you, it's not cold. So I did. I tied the laces around my neck and stuffed my socks in my pockets, and then we really did saunter, the pair of us. The grass was cool and springy under my feet, and it looked navy-blue in the moonlight. It was like being in a film, you know, one of those old black-and-white musicals, where people suddenly start hugging lamp-posts and bursting into a duet. It would have taken very little to persuade me to hug a lamp-post. I felt game for anything. I think it's the moon that does it.

When we got home, the flat smelt of garam masala, which is

not very romantic, but we made some hot chocolate and we put on a bar of the electric fire, not because it was cold, but more for the glow, and then we turned the lights off and lit some candles. We sat up for ages in the candlelight and toasted our toes at the fire, and sometimes we talked and sometimes we were silent, except for the soft hiss of the electric fire and the occasional sputtering of the candles. And the best part was that Imelda didn't try to make me talk about Mum, which I had been just a bit afraid of. We didn't talk about anything much, except the film we'd seen, and how the moon looked, dropped into the canal like that. Like a Japanese picture.

I never once thought of Dad and Margaret and what they must be doing. Not until this morning.

We slept late. Imelda never goes to church, not even at Christmas, which is a bit extreme, I must say, though it has the value of consistency, I suppose. She says she is an apostate, which sounds like something holy, but is actually the exact opposite. It must have been nearly mid-day when we got up. Time for brunch, Imelda announced, and said I could choose between going to a jazz brunch in a pub in town or Bewley's. Do you eat *every* day in Bewley's? I asked. She shrugged and said nearly every day. I know it sounds silly, but to me at that moment it seemed the height of sophistication to live in a flat and eat in Bewley's most days, and I longed to be grown up and finished my education so I could live like that too.

I'm not really into jazz, though I keep that to myself — it's terribly uncool not to be into jazz — so I chose Bewley's. But as soon as I sat down to my plate of sausages and scrambled eggs I started to cry. Mum used to make scrambled eggs when I was little and heap them up on toast, just like that. I know it doesn't sound

very spiritual, getting doleful over a plate of scrambled egg, but life is like that, you know, it's not a romantic novel after all.

So anyway, as Lisa always says every time she starts a new paragraph, so to speak, in any story she is telling, there I was plopping big fat tears onto my brunch, and with my shoulders heaving unbecomingly. Imelda made soothing noises as best she could and through my tears I picked up her cutlery and started cutting up her sausages for her. I must have looked a bit peculiar, leaning across the table and doing that, with tears running down my nose and onto the brawny table-top. I suddenly had a vision of myself doing it, how ridiculous I must have looked, and that made me giggle, so I cheered up a little then. But having broached the subject, so to speak, by crying, I then began to get emotional about Dad and Margaret too and the fact that they had gone off on this weekend, and I told Imelda I thought he might have the decency to wait till Mum was cold in her grave — I don't know what made me use such a horrible expression, but of course as soon as I said it, I realised the awfulness of it, and that made me cry some more. I got angry then, and I let fly about Dad and his callousness. I forget sometimes that Imelda is his sister, but I don't think she goes in for false loyalty anyway. She sat and listened, and chewed her sausages thoughtfully. She didn't say anything. She didn't stand up for Dad, but she didn't tell me to pull myself together either. I could have kissed her for the way she just listened and chewed like that. I would have too, if it hadn't been Bewley's on a Sunday morning, and the scrambled eggs and everything.

Wednesday 16th July

He's finally admitted that he wants Milly-Molly-Mandy (I'm really going to have to stop calling her that) to move in with us.

Well, he didn't actually put it like that. He said he was 'serious' about Margaret, and he wants me to know this, as we will have to start to plan for the future, but I knew what he meant. I threw a tantrum. Well, I felt I owed it to Mum. It was quite a spectacular tantrum. I smashed two dinner plates and a bottle of ink. Dad quietly swept up the shards, but he couldn't do much about the ink, except dab at it with kitchen paper. It made an amazing pattern on the wallpaper, like one of those psychological tests. What does this ink spot say to you? Treachery? Inconstancy? Adultery even? Not technically, perhaps, but as near as makes no difference, and anyway, who says not? This relationship has developed suspiciously quickly. It's still there. The inkspot, I mean.

It really needled him, not the inkspot specifically, the tantrum in general, I could see that. He came to my room afterwards, when I was sprawled prone on my bed, with my hair all over the duvet, all passion spent, just sobbing occasionally. He sat very tentatively on the edge of the bed and spoke softly to me, as if I were a small child. He stroked my hair. Then he started to gather it all up, like a skein of wool, and he wound it around his wrists. (It's pretty long.) I couldn't be sure, because my face was firmly in the pillow, but I think at one point he may have raised it to his lips. We sat there for ages like that, and then he said, If it makes you so unhappy, Cindy, OK, let's forget it.

Not on your life! You can't just 'forget' something like that. I'm not going to let him away with it that easily. I turned over and shook my hair free. I mumbled, No, it was all right, it was his house, his life, if he wanted to share it with someone from outside the family, that was his business. He winced when I said the bit about someone outside the family, and he started to protest that of course it was my house too, my home, and he wouldn't dream

of forcing me to share it with other people, it was just that he felt the house was so empty with only the two of us, and that I needed company, and wouldn't it be nice to have two girls of my own age about the place. Talk about naive! Or maybe it wasn't so much naive. Maybe it was straightforward manipulation. It was like a scene from one of those very bad, very mushy Hollywood films, one of the ones we sometimes get out on video on a Sunday evening and have a giggle over. *Sleepless in Seattle* maybe, or *Kramer versus Kramer*.

That gave me an idea, so I said that it would be so much easier if Dad and Mum were divorced, that then I could just go and live with Mum, but that being an orphan, I didn't have that option, and that's what made it so difficult for me. Divorce made him wince again. I knew it would. And orphan really cracked him up. He started to cry quietly. He put his hand to his forehead and wept.

He's not urbane now, I thought.

Thursday 24th July

Margaret has broken it off! She says Dad is too recently widowed (should it not be widowered for a man? and if not, why not?), and is not in any position to make a radical life decision at the moment. I know that's just her potted psychologist self talking, but at least it's a reprieve. Maybe she isn't a total nerd.

Dad is a broken man.

Friday 25th July

Dad's booked two tickets to Lisbon for a fortnight, leaving tomorrow! They're for me and him, by the way, not him and Margaret.

Dad and I had a wonderful holiday! I thought it might be a strain, just the two of us, but it wasn't. The weather was baking, far too hot for my black gear, which was all I had, as we left in such a rush, so on the first day Dad took me to a department store and bought me three cotton dresses, all long and pale, a straw hat and a pair of flat strappy sandals. After that I waltzed around on his arm, like a Helena Bonham-Carter character in one of those Edwardian films. Not that I am as pretty as Helena Bonham-Carter, and glasses aren't really in role, but still, with my straw bonnet well down on my head, I would pass at an angle anyway. Besides, I had my contact lenses for good wear.

We visited art galleries and churches and palaces by day, fabulous places, with the most gorgeous tiling you can imagine, and then every evening we sought out a new restaurant and ate fresh sardines and swordfish and goat and swigged red wine, sitting at little rickety tables out of doors, on pavements and terraces. Sometimes they cooked the sardines on an outdoor brazier. We sat around and ate lots of bitter little pinkish-black olives that they brought to us on platters while we waited for our orders to cook. They served cheese also as an *hors d'oeuvre*, sharp-tasting but creamy-textured white cheese, with the olives usually. Some evenings we had African dishes, a legacy of the Portuguese colonial past. That's where the goat came in, I think.

We hear so much about how poor Portugal is nowadays, that it is hard to remember it was once such a colonial power. Lisbon is weird like that, all these really fabulous palaces and so on, and then if you take the train anywhere you can see the backs of the houses, slum-houses really, with the washing hanging dolefully

out of the windows. It makes you wonder how dirty the clothes were *before* they were washed, when you see the state of them on the line.

We went to Sintra one day. That's a really pretty village outside Lisbon, in the hills. And Estoril, we went there another day, very fashionable, very European, which sounds ridiculous, but I mean you could pretend you were in Baden-Baden, if you see what I mean, or on the Lido, watching old who's-it in *Death in Venice* with his make-up melting. You could even be a William Trevor character, or a hesitant Anita Brookner middle-aged girl. (I'm quite well read, you will observe. English is my best subject, not all thanks to Mr O'Donnell. There is some honest-to-god natural talent there too.)

Dad was great in Portugal. It was like old times, except for Mum not being there of course. But I didn't miss her as much as you'd expect. We even went to a casino one night. Now was that Estoril or Cascais? I can't remember. I took off my straw hat for that, and put my hair up, to look older. It was delicious having Dad all to myself, not having to listen in on the extension to make sure it's not Margaret again. He did slip away a couple of times, ostensibly to change traveller's cheques, but I knew he was really ringing her. I know she broke it off, but I don't imagine she forbade him to ring her. It didn't seem to matter so much, when I knew he was on a post office phone and there was probably a queue outside and a Portuguese telephonist listening in to improve his English.

I hated coming home. It is always either raining at Dublin Airport or has just been raining, or it's working itself up to rain again. It's as though the holiday people arrange it that way so that you want to rush out and book your next holiday as soon as you

step off the plane. Maybe they have a secret arrangement with the Met office to leave one of those little cloudburst stickers they use on the TV weather forecast permanently in place at Collinstown, and maybe it works by a sort of voodoo.

Thursday 14th August

I went over to Lisa's, to bring her her present, a tile from Sintra, which is where they make them. She looked at it and said, What am I supposed to do with a single tile? Tile the shower in the kids' dolls-house? Very witty, very amusing, I don't think. It's really an exceptionally pretty tile, with a picture of a bird painted on it in lovely colours. I said it was just a token, that it was only for decoration, and she said she knew that, she was just pulling my leg. You know that sinking feeling you get in Dublin Airport when you come home from your holidays, I got it all over again at Lisa's place today.

We went to the Phoenix Park then. That was complicated. Lisa's little brother Trevor is learning to cycle, so Lisa cycled his bicycle over, and I got the bus with Trevor. He wriggled on the seat all the way and chewed gum. I am beginning to see the disadvantages of younger brothers. I don't see why it had to be the Phoenix Park. What's wrong with all the parks on the south side? But apparently Trevor wanted to use the cycle paths in the Phoeno and nothing else would do him. He couldn't cycle there himself, as he is not safe to let out on the road yet, which is why Lisa had to cycle his bike there for him.

Once we got there it was fine, because he cycled off on his own, wobbled off I should say, and Lisa and I got to sit on a park bench under a tree and watch the world go by. It sort of glided by. There were all these people on their bikes, sailing along the cycle paths,

not like Ireland at all, more like Holland, and people on roller-blades on the pedestrian paths, and then the cars on the main road. Everyone seemed to be rolling along on some sort of wheels, in the afternoon sunlight. It was a bit like being a figure in a modern-day, summery version of those winter scenes you see in the Dutch sections of art galleries, with bright knots of colour that are people skating on the canals. Sitting on our bench with everyone spinning along, in and out of our field of vision, calling to each other, and dogs leaping over fences in the distance, it all seemed a bit unreal.

Lisa seemed very low – the comment about the tile was not in character – so I asked her what was up. Then it all came out, that her mum was pregnant again. I couldn't see what the problem was. She said it was ridiculous having six children in this day and age, and had her parents no shame? That they were old enough to be grandparents. They're only about forty, actually, but I suppose she is technically correct. I asked was *she*... She said, Don't be stupid, I have more sense – more than my mum anyway. Well, I don't know, she has a boyfriend, nominally anyway, though she hardly ever seems to go out with him. His name is Kieran. In theory I go along with old Iron Knickers (our RE teacher) that it's more 'mature', not to mention infinitely more hygienic, not to sleep with your boyfriend when you're our age. I hope that if the opportunity arose, I would make the mature decision.

I couldn't really pin Lisa down about what the problem is. Maybe she is jealous. Maybe she does really think she is the one who should be having babies but won't admit it. But she says she just thinks it is disgusting people of her parents' age having sex. You'd think they were wrinklies and dribblies altogether the way

she talks. There I was worrying that my parents' sexual relationship had broken down, and Lisa has the opposite worry. Is there
no end to the problems parents cause? Who'd be a teenager? You
don't even have to be in love for it to be a nightmare. Actually,
maybe if you were in love, it might even be a bit better. It'd be a
bit of a distraction from all the other rubbish you have to deal with.
Maybe I should try it. Though I don't actually know all that many
boys.

Anyway, I forgave Lisa for being narky about the tile when I
heard what was on her mind, even though it's a lovely tile and I'd
just as soon have it back if she doesn't want it.

Thursday, 21st August

I should have known. I should have known this just wasn't going
to go away. Dad and Margaret are back together again. I knew that
break-up was just a tactical move, just as, I suppose, Dad taking
me off on holiday was a counter-tactic. And now we've been
invited to Sunday lunch at their house, to seal the bond I suppose.
I can't imagine anything more ghastly. I'm sure they just have
some very ordinary little place with oversized windows and an
open-plan front garden. They're all like that in Ballywhatsit,
where they live, the ones with double-glazing looking down their
noses at the rest, and a bunch of token detached ones in a special
snobs' cul-de-sac for £10,000 extra. Not a decent architrave between them, but lots of very deep wallpaper borders used at
dado-rail level, for an old-fashioned look. It's bound to have a
horrid little nest of tables, I just know it, and a breakfast bar. I bet
Dad wants them to move in together again, though he has carefully avoided mentioning the subject. He is probably fondly
imagining his accumulated issues of *The Great Composers* nestling

in her teak-effect magazine rack right now. Ugh!

Well, I'm just not going, and I told him so. I said I'd go to lunch all right, but that he needn't think he was going to persuade me to move in there with that lot. I said *he* could move in if he liked. He said not to be ridiculous, he hadn't a notion of moving in with them, and even if he was, he certainly wasn't going to do it without me. Well, of course it was ridiculous, but logic really wasn't the point.

Friday 29th August

Hey! I've just had a really amazing idea. Maybe it wasn't so ridiculous after all to suggest Dad moves out. If he did, I'd have to have someone come and live with me, and Imelda is the obvious candidate. I know she has this really cool flat and all, but she'd have much more space here, and it needn't be for ever, just till I'm old enough – or until Dad comes to his senses and moves back. I'll ask her tomorrow, just whether she'd be agreeable in principle. The more I think about this, the more I like it. It could be such fun!

Saturday 30th August

Imelda didn't think it was such a great idea. Actually, it was a bit embarrassing. She tried to let me down gently, but she said she had her own life to lead, and while I was very welcome to come and visit and stay for weekends and stuff, that really her lifestyle and mine wouldn't 'mingle' in the long term. I never imagined Imelda as having a lifestyle before, apart from going to Bewley's and the deadly taps and all that. I wonder if lifestyle's a code word for sex life? Oh god! Everyone seems to have one of those, except me.

Oh, well, anyway, maybe it won't arise. Dad hasn't mentioned anything more about moving out or having them move in for a whole week. Maybe he's gone off the idea, or maybe he's just decided to drop it for the moment. In fact, he hasn't mentioned anything very much for ages. He seems, oh, I don't know, preoccupied. Maybe things are tough at work. Maybe he has more important things to think about.

Monday 1st September

Back to school today. Something of a relief, really, after the turbulent summer I've been having. Well, it may not look turbulent on the outside, but it feels turbulent. Why don't I just behave turbulent, like a normal teenager – take ecstasy, get a nose-ring, go shoplifting? That'd teach him to mess me around like this. But I suppose I am just too sensible and mature for my own good.

We had lunch yesterday *chez* the Magees. I got dressed up for it. I put on one of the dresses Dad bought me in Lisbon, a really pretty one in sort of *café-au-lait* cotton with a tiny cornflower-blue pattern, mid-calf length and button-down-the-front, that sort of swings when I walk – something to do with the way it's cut, I think. It makes it look as if I've got breasts. Well, I have, of course, but they're not much to get excited about. I wore my hair in a tortoise-shell barette and put on the straw hat too, to complete the effect. All that was missing was the parasol.

You know, I thought Dad would like it that I dressed up for his lady love and her brats, but can you imagine what he said? He said there was no need to be so dramatic. Dramatic! Since when is putting on a nice summer dress being dramatic? I know dozens of parents who would be delighted if their daughters would wear something other than jeans. (Actually, part of the reason I got

dressed up is that my black outfit is too filthy to recycle for even one more day, but there's no need for him to know that.) Anyway, I said I'd leave off the straw hat if that would make him happier. He said yes, it would be less of a statement. I don't know what he meant about a statement. Anyone would think I was going in a bodystocking or a basque, the way he looked at me. Maybe it was the eyeshadow and lipstick he didn't like, but he didn't say so and I don't think it was overdone. Plum, the lipstick is called. It's a sort of browny purple and good with really pale skin like mine. Maybe that's what he meant by dramatic.

Anyway, the house wasn't as bad as I imagined it. It was pretty ugly from the outside all right, except that she has all these lovely rosebushes in the front, but inside it was quite homey and comfortable, in a boring sort of way, of course. I was gratified to see they had an elaborate magazine rack, as predicted, but it was in that honey pine you see everywhere these days.

The food was wonderful, proper steak-and-kidney pie with home-made pastry and real egg crème caramel to follow. I told Margaret how good it was. There is no point in begrudgery after all. Margaret looked a bit pale, I thought, and she swallowed even more often and more audibly than usual. Maybe she is feeling the strain. That is only to be expected.

There was wine, but I didn't have any, as I didn't want to end up on Dún Laoghaire pier again. One of the Magee girls had half-a-thimbleful, Magee *mère* didn't have any, not even when pressed by Dad – come to think of it, she didn't eat much either – so Dad ended up having the bottle to himself. He never drinks too much, but he had three glasses, which is way over the limit for driving, so then we had to sit around for hours until he sobered up.

After lunch Ashling and Alva washed up. I would have offered to help, only I was embarrassed, but it was just as embarrassing to sit on at the table while Dad sipped his third glass of wine and fiddled with his tie-pin – I regret to say, he is the sort of man that wears a tie-pin, even on a Sunday – and Margaret tried to make smalltalk with me. She asked me who my favourite popgroup is, typical adult question to a teenager, a bit like asking a child what class they're in. I bet the two Magees are into Boyzone. I bet they have posters blu-tacked to their bedroom walls. I said I didn't follow pop, and do you know what she offered in reply to that? Remember that Margaret Magee is a remarkably unintelligent woman. She said, you've guessed, that that was very interesting. It is not very interesting. It is not even mildly interesting. It is merely a fact, and not a remarkable fact. Lots of teenagers don't follow pop just as lots of over-sixties don't play bingo. I refrained from saying this, which I think shows remarkable self-control. I can be very self-controlled at times.

It was a relief when the girls came back from the kitchen. I never thought I would see the day when I would be glad to see that pair. Ashling suggested a game of Monopoly. Monopoly! Can you imagine me playing Monopoly? But I did. I didn't want to be difficult. It wasn't bad. I was the banker, and I won.

Tuesday 2nd September

Old Gravyface came bobbing up to me in the corridor today and shook my hand. Teachers never do that. I didn't know how to take it. His hand was very knobbly and damp, like a bag of odd-sized marbles wrapped up in a dishcloth. He asked me if I had had a good summer, and how I was feeling. I said something polite. It's a bit difficult making smalltalk with a teacher, especially when

they have to crane their neck to look up at you. I didn't realise how much I must have grown over the summer.

Meeting him reminded me that it is going to be very awkward meeting Milly-Molly-Mandy in school. I've managed to avoid her so far. I didn't even see her in assembly this morning, which is odd.

Thursday 4th September

Still no sign of Margaret at assembly. That's really the only place I am likely to come across her, I've decided, as long as I don't get sent to the staffroom for something. Maybe I can keep out of her way all term, with a little bit of forward thinking.

Saturday 6th September

Managed to avoid Margaret all week in school.

Lisa says her mum is going all mushy, now that she's past the sick stage. She says it was brutal when she was getting sick in the mornings, but she thinks the mushy stage is worse. I really think she is being a bit silly about all this. Why doesn't she just enjoy the whole thing? It will be lovely to have a new baby in the house. I said I would go over and help her to mind it when it was born. She snorted at that, which is really not a very attractive sound.

Dad is still very *distrait*. I hope he hasn't got financial worries. I read somewhere that fathers worry about financial security a lot, and that if they are out-of-sorts or aloof, it is probably some sort of business worry. This sounds a bit sexist to me, but you never know.

Monday 8th September

Finally saw Milly-Molly-Mandy at school. I'm kind of glad, really, as I was dreading it, and now it's over and it wasn't too bad. I was crossing over to the science lab, which is in a separate building from the main school, and she seemed to be coming in late. I think it was about 11 o'clock. By the time I'd spotted her it was too late to hide or pretend I hadn't seen her, so I sort of half-smiled at her. She gave me a little wave as she locked her car. I was glad I was on my own. If any of the others had seen the little wave, they might have put two and two together and got about fifteen. Not even Lisa knows that Dad came close to moving in with her this summer. She was wearing a very girlish sort of frock, I thought, with one of those things I think you call a yoke, with a silly ribbon tied in a bow at the front. I noticed, because she's usually in little grey business skirts and polyester blouses. Maybe Dad is making her feel young. Yuck! But I noted with satisfaction that her hair has gone rather limp. Her topiary haircut has gone out of shape because of this, and she looks less like a bay tree and more like a raggy old bush.

Monday 15th September

Junior Cert results came out today. I got five A's and three B's. Mr Garvey shook my hand again, his knobbly adam's apple going ape in his throat, even though I only got a B in maths. Mr O'Donnell congratulated me too, as well he might – A's in English don't grow on trees. We found out his first name is Hugh, like the historical Hugh O'Donnell, and Lisa nicknamed him Red Hugh, not because of his hair (which is black and curly), but because of the way he blushes when he talks to you. Red Hugh was very

pleased with my result, judging by the shade of crimson he went. I would have been cheesed off if I hadn't got an A, actually, but you can't say that sort of thing.

Lisa wants me to go out with the rest tonight, to celebrate. I hate that sort of thing, but she's been nagging at me, so maybe I will, just this once.

Wednesday 17th September

Yesterday was the worst day of my life. I didn't go out with the others after all on Monday night, but I still woke up with what felt like a hangover – something I have never had, I hasten to add, I'm just going by other people's descriptions. I think it must have been a bug, but I'd never have convinced anyone it was if I'd been out the night before. All I did was just sit in and watch TV with Dad. We hardly ever do that. It was quite cosy actually. It was the first time I felt really close to him since Mum died, even including the holiday, which was fun but a bit unreal after all. We didn't do anything special to celebrate the exam results, but at eleven o'clock we made tea and had gingersnaps with it. We dunked the gingersnaps in the tea until they started to melt. We both had to get fresh cups at one point because we had such a lot of wet gingersnap swirling around in our tea like disintegrating cotton wool with tentacles that it was undrinkable. After that we watched a late night movie. Dad had a can of lager and I had some flat Coke I found in the dining room. Not exactly a champagne party, but I don't mind flat Coke.

Maybe it was the Coke that did it, now I come to think of it, although I don't think Coke can really go off. Anyway, in the morning I really felt rotten. Dad called me when I didn't appear for breakfast. He knocked on my door and put his head around it

to ask if I was going to get up. He took one look at me and pronounced me unfit for school. Then he disappeared and came back with a cup of coffee. I took a sniff at it and my stomach turned right over and I broke out in a sweat. Dad disappeared again and came back with a cup of tea, very weak, very hot, very sweet, and I managed to sip at that. He sat at the edge of the bed and watched me. I finished the tea and gave him a little smile. He said, That's my girl. Then he brought me a basin and a towel, just in case, and a bottle of Ballygowan, and said he'd come home at lunchtime, to see how I was doing. He was so sweet, it was nearly worth being ill to have him be so attentive to me. He can be very nice sometimes, in spite of everything. It is very fine of me to admit that, when you consider what happened later.

It was at lunchtime he dropped his bombshell. I had slept, after he left, till about noon. Then I had a shower, which made me feel much better – I never actually got sick – and wandered around for a bit in my bathrobe, wondering what to wear. Most of my usual gear was in the wash, and I didn't feel up to the demands of a dress. Then I had a bright idea. I don't know why I never thought of it before. Mum's clothes were still in her wardrobe and in the drawers of her dressing table. I went in there and rummaged around. It was kind of sad to see them all folded away so neatly, just waiting to be worn. I must do a proper sort through them some day and decide what I want to keep, and what should go to the Oxfam shop. Anyway, I found a rather nice tracksuit, in a sort of rosy red colour she was fond of. When I put the top over my head, I got a waft of her perfume, except it was a bit musty. It made my scalp prickle.

Then I went down to the kitchen and started to get the lunch. I was still feeling pretty queasy, but I remembered there was some

54

potato soup in the freezer, and I thought I could face that, so I got it out and started to heat it up. It takes a ridiculous length of time to defrost soup. You would have a fresh soup made from scratch while you're waiting for it. Anyway, there I was, standing at the stove, endlessly stirring this soup-iceberg with a wooden spoon, trying to chip bits off the main lump and sort of smear it around the bottom of the saucepan, to speed things up. I don't know if doing that helps, but it's something to do other than biting your fingernails. As I stood there, I heard Dad's key in the lock. Hi there! I chirruped, through the open kitchen door, and I could see him stopping dead in the hallway. What's wrong? I called out. He shook himself out of his torpor then and hung his keys up on the little key-hook by the front door, and then he came on into the kitchen.

He sat down quietly at the kitchen table and said, For a minute there, I thought you were your mother. This was stretching things a bit. I know I was wearing her tracksuit, but I am a completely different shape from her, and I am as dark as she was fair. I have some news for you, Cindy, he said in a very low voice, not like his usual brash self at all. I stopped stirring and went and sat opposite him, a wave of nausea rippling through my body. I don't know if it was the tail end of the bug – my mouth still felt as if it was lined with steel wool – or if it was apprehension.

I put my elbows on the table and rested my cheeks in my upturned hands on purpose so that I could easily close my fingers over my face if I thought I was going to flush with fear or anger or embarrassment. I felt I needed to be ready for all contingencies. This sounded serious. I thought he might be going to bring up the question of moving in with Margaret again, or her moving in here.

Which, in a sense, he did, only more so, really. He told me that Margaret is pregnant, and that in view of that they have decided to get married next month. I was so stunned that I forgot to throw a tantrum, and by the time I thought of it, it was too late. The moment had passed. I just sat there, my fingers stretched across my face and my eyes smarting. It wasn't tears. I didn't feel tearful. I didn't even feel sad or angry, just stunned, but I felt as if the surfaces of my eyes were cold. I blinked slowly a few times, drawing my eyelids down over my eyes to warm them up. I don't know how long I just sat there staring at him, blinking and opening my eyes again, but it must have been quite a while, because the next thing I was aware of was the soup burning.

I don't know why he chose that moment to tell me. What really kills me is that while we were messing around with gingersnaps and giggling over the movie, he had known this all the time. At least, I assume he must have. He hardly heard it yesterday morning and came right home and told me at lunchtime. Anyway, it ruined everything for me. I felt let down, like a balloon somebody has just let the air out of.

Friday 19th September

I am still stunned. I can hardly believe this. How can grown-up people let this sort of thing happen? And to think they have the nerve to tell us how to behave! They are always rattling on in our school about how an unplanned pregnancy (they won't say unwanted pregnancy, because that goes against the Catholic ethos) can really mess up your life. And she's a *guidance counsellor*, not just any old teacher. There is a pro-adoption policy in our school. When anyone gets pregnant – I don't mean it happens all the time, but it has happened – she is advised (a) not to marry the

father, on the grounds that (i) they are too young and (ii) a pregnancy is a very bad reason for marriage, and (b) not to try to bring up the child herself, as that is supposed to damage her career propects. Well, they don't put it like that, they say something like interrupt her education, but that's what they mean. How can Milly-Molly-Mandy possibly go around giving out the party line on that one with her belly sticking out into the middle of next week, and a brand new wedding ring on her finger? How come pregnancy is a bad reason to get married if you are sixteen, but really the only reason if you are forty? And is forty not too old to be getting pregnant anyway? This situation has irresponsible written all over it. I bet she did it on purpose, to snare him, the cow.

She'll have to resign. Not that the nuns would make her. That would damage their liberal reputation. But her credibility is going to be zilch after this one.

Saturday 20th September

I have to sit down very carefully several times a day and tell myself that we are going to have a baby in this house, and it's not just any old baby, this is my half-sister or -brother we are talking about. Not to mention the other additions to this family — a stepmother and two stepsisters. That is four new people in my family virtually at the drop of a hat, just as I am getting used to being two people instead of three. It's not fair. Especially when you think how obnoxious the other three are. Not that they're mean or horrible or anything, just plain boring and neurotic and silly and, oh, just not like *us*. Of course, we're neurotic too, everyone is, but I do think *our* neuroses are more creative.

Oh Mum! I wish you could come back from wherever it is dead people go to and tell him this is your house, he is your husband,

you are my mother. That is the way things are *meant* to be, not this awful mixed-up mess of a botched family, all steps and halves. I wouldn't ever sneer at your Colour me Beautiful theories or your wine-tasting evenings or any of your silly, oh-so-Mum-like pretensions ever again. I'd stop telling you not to be so American. I'd never correct your spelling or your table manners, I promise I wouldn't. Why is this all happening to me? What did I do to deserve it? I know I am not the nicest person in the world, but I'm not actively evil, am I?

Monday 22nd September

I told Lisa at the weekend. She put her hand across her mouth and let a yelp, to show how amazed she was, but I don't really think she was all that shocked really. She was just doing it for effect. She admitted then that she has suspected all along. It's easy to say that afterwards, but she pointed out that Milly-Molly-Mandy had skipped assembly every morning so far this term, and that she had started to wear looser clothes, and her skin had got blotchy. I stared at that, but she said she read it in a book. I had a funny feeling listening to her. She made it all seem so clinical. I suppose she's lived through a lot of her mother's pregnancies. Maybe it's thickened her skin. Still, I found myself doing the same thing, adding up the wine Margaret didn't have at lunch that day, her pale complexion, Dad's preoccupation in recent weeks. It all began to make sense, horrible, twisted sense, but logical all the same.

I don't know how far gone she is. I don't want to know when this calamitous event is going to happen. And I particularly don't want to know, don't want even to think about, when this wretched child was conceived. Was it before or after Lisbon, for example?

Why do I even ask myself that? I don't want to know. Yet I can't stop wondering, poking at it they way you keep passing your tongue over a new filling in one of your teeth, or you can't help picking a scab off a cut or zapping a zit. Even her hair going limp like that is supposed to be a sign, according to Lisa. Very worldly-wise is our Lisa.

It'll be lovely, though, said Lisa slyly, having a new baby in the house. I'll come over and help you to mind it if you like. With friends like that... and you know the rest.

Monday 29th September

The wedding is in three weeks time. In three weeks I will have a stepmother, not a wicked stepmother, but rather a stupid one, which is probably worse. In three weeks I will have two unbearably stupid stepsisters. And in five and a half months I will have a new half-sibling. I don't know how I am going to cope with all of this. Is there a book out there that tells you what the protocol is in these situations? Not that I really want to know the protocol. Protocol is what you follow when you want to behave well. I don't. I want to behave horribly badly, but I probably won't. I'm just too well brought up.

I haven't met the terrible duo, A and A Magee, since the dreadful news, but according to Dad they are ecstatic about the baby. I'm sure he said that to make me feel bad that I'm not over the moon about this whole stinking situation too, the ratbag.

Tuesday 30th September

They're all busy planning the wedding – Dad is on the phone every evening – but does anyone actually think about what it is

going to be like afterwards, in this newly forged family? (Forged is a strangely appropriate term, now I come to think of it.) How on earth are we all going to get on together?

I made Dad sit down last night and tell me his plans in detail. I actually made an appointment with him, as otherwise I felt he would just go around avoiding the issue. It is only going to be in the registry office – the wedding, I mean – because of her being divorced, I suppose, and he promised there won't be a big fuss. They aren't going in for bridesmaids in taffeta and a tiered cake and all the bit. At least, Dad says they aren't, but I can't see that Ashling and Alva passing up a chance to wear floral headbands and white gloves. Well, if they do turn this into a ProNuptia circus, I will just refuse to go. I did consider refusing to go anyway, but Imelda says that would be too hard on Dad. Still, I reserve the right not to go if it all gets too awful, and I told him so.

Then I went on and said that when I wanted to know about his plans, I wasn't really thinking about the wedding, I was thinking about life. I asked him who was going to live where, and how it was all going to work out in practice. He looked very uncomfortable when I asked him this. That was rather satisfying. I'm beginning to think that making appointments is more beneficial in the long run than throwing tantrums. I realise this is a mature approach on my part. Somebody has to be mature around here. Anyway, the most I could get out of him was that the Magees are going to move in with us. She is going to put her house on the market as soon as the wedding is over. I reminded him, very soberly, very unemotionally, very factually, that he said a few weeks ago that this was my home and he wasn't going to move people into it unless I agreed. He looked doubly uncomfortable at this and he actually said he was sorry. That was a deeply

satisfying moment, but that sort of satisfaction doesn't last. The situation remains the same. He said lamely that the circumstances had changed, and that he couldn't very well do anything about it now, after all there is a baby to think of. Very convenient this baby is turning out to be.

Wednesday 8th October

I've been trying to imagine what it's going to be like, and I don't much like what I imagine – *her* cooking in our kitchen, watching our TV, talking – swallowing – on our phone, her slippers under Mum's side of the bed, her brats sprawling on our sofa, her Tampax in our bathroom cupboard, the hairs from her hairbrush nestling in our bin.

I think I'd better sort through Mum's clothes right away. It's bad enough to think of her home being defiled, but at least I can protect some of her things. I couldn't bear to think of Margaret opening a drawer and shoving Mum's blouses and things to one side to make room for her horrible polyester things.

Thursday 9th October

I have just been struck by a most pernicious and awful thought. This baby will be *their* half-sibling too. Gross! 'Stepsisters' has a comfortingly remote sound to it, but stepsisters who are half-sisters to my half-sibling are practically family. Oh Mum! I don't wish you were here, because that would be just too complicated, but I wish I had a mum all the same. I need one just now. Lisa is practically useless – I think she is just so titillated by the whole business that she can't function as a best friend is supposed to, and anyway, she has her own mum to worry about – and even

Imelda doesn't really understand. No, that's not fair, I think she understands all right, but there isn't much she can do about it really, except be there. And she's being there all right. She rings me every day, and we spend a lot of time together at weekends. Sometimes she comes over here for dinner, and sometimes I go and stay the night at her place. I'm glad she's there. At least somebody in this family is dependable.

Friday 17th October

She's really starting to show. You'd think she would get a corset or something. It's embarrassing at school. Some of the girls are starting to notice. Somebody said fifth year have opened a book on who the father is. Mr Gravy is even money, and Fr Egan is three to one. That's really mean. Fr Egan isn't like that. They're just doing it to be daring, and because it's fashionable to accuse priests of that sort of thing. If only they knew! Well, I suppose they will soon enough. I'm not going to be able to keep hidden the fact that one of the teachers has married my dad and is about to have his baby.

It's all very well for Ashling and Alva. They're in a different school. Probably nobody at their school suspects a thing. Sometimes I wish I could just crawl away and hibernate and then when I woke up it would all have unhappened. I don't mean Mum dying. I know that's not going to unhappen. But the rest — maybe it will all turn out to be a horrible mistake. Maybe Dad will get sense. Maybe there'll be a blue moon.

One thing for sure, I am never going to get pregnant unless I am well and truly happily married. Or maybe I'll just be a nun and not have anything to do with that scum known as the male of the species.

The wedding was yesterday. Ashling and Alva weren't actually bridesmaids. Dad said it wouldn't be fair if I couldn't be. Margaret said I could be, it was just that I wouldn't, and Dad said that it came to the same thing. That was the first time he stood up for me for ages. Maybe he is beginning to regret this whole affair. Well, it's too late now. Ha! I could make a sage little remark about making your bed and lying in it, but that would be just a little bit too literal in the circumstances.

I didn't go in the end. I promised myself I wouldn't if Ashling and Alva were going to go as geisha girls, and they did (Ashling actually wore a string of pearls), but it wasn't that really. I just couldn't face it in the end. I told Dad so at breakfast, the day before the wedding. I said I was sorry, but I didn't think I could make it. He went white. For a moment I forgot how cross and upset I was and that this is all entirely his own doing and his own fault and I almost felt sorry for him. But I went on spooning up my cornflakes (yes, cornflakes – Dad's been too preoccupied lately to bother with his elaborate breakfasts) and I didn't say anything for a bit. Then he sighed a very long, elaborate, *planned* sort of sigh, and said it was up to me, he couldn't force me. I said I wasn't doing it to be mean (though a tiny part of me knew that wasn't true) it was just that I couldn't face it (that part *was* true, though – feelings are so complicated aren't they?), and he said that was OK, and then I went around to his side of the table and stood behind his chair and gave him a little backwards sort of hug. He patted my hand and didn't say anything, but I think that meant he forgave me for not going, which is only fair – after all it is my prerogative. I don't have to actively participate in this whole sorry

affair. It's bad enough having the Magees thrust into intimacy with me against my will, without my having to be there, cheering them all on at the signing of the contract.

Imelda was one witness, and Fr Egan was the other. He went along, even though it was a registry office wedding, which I think was pretty sporting of him. I could never truly respect a man who spends every Saturday of his life polishing his Toyota or Mazda or whatever it is, but still, he's decent enough. Maybe I really will be a nun.

I thought about going to school yesterday, treating it like any other day, but then I thought why give up the chance of a perfectly good day off, so instead I stayed in bed until Dad had left the house in his corduroy jacket and second-best shirt — he was careful not to overdo it, so as not to offend me more than strictly necessary. Big deal.

Then I got up and sort of mooched around for a bit, but I couldn't get it out of mind what was going on in Molesworth Street. In the end I hopped on a bus and went and stood around outside the registry office. (I know it's correctly the register office, but nobody actually says that, and I am working on not being pedantic. I think it is important to recognise one's faults and work to eliminate them. If everyone took that attitude, the world would be a pleasanter place.)

I felt a bit goofy hanging around, and for one wild moment I thought I might pop down to Read's on Nassau Street and buy a packet of confetti, but then I thought that would be a bit inconsistent. I sort of kicked my heels for a while, and in the end I decided it was a bad idea to have come, so I went off to Waterstone's and had a good poke around the poetry section, which is usually very consoling. But it wasn't all that consoling yesterday,

and at one point when I was trying to read a poem about Seamus Heaney's mother dying I couldn't read it properly, the words kept getting fuzzed up and sort of sliding around the page, and then I realised that the reason was that I was crying. I slid the little book back between the others on the shelf – poetry books are always so elegantly slim – and slunk out of the shop before someone saw me and tried to be kind. I didn't think I could bear it if anyone asked what was wrong. Not that it was very likely really. People don't. Grief embarrasses people. They pretend they don't want to embarrass you by not letting on they've seen your grief, but really it is themselves they don't want to embarrass.

I reckoned they must be well and truly married by then, so I went to catch the bus home. But standing there at the bus-stop in the cold, I had a sudden impulse and I caught another bus instead, hardly knowing what I was doing. I sat on the top deck all by myself and blew my nose privately, and looked out of the window at all the people scurrying around, shopping as if their lives depended on it, as if shopping was a valid thing to do with your life, but instead of feeling superior to them as I usually do when I notice the shallowness of other people (which is quite often, I have to admit), I just felt immensely sorry for them all, imagining that they were probably all shopping so they wouldn't have to do anything more real. Which is a load of sentimental hogwash, I know. Half of them probably weren't shopping at all. They were probably just buying stamps or running out of the office to snatch an early lunch or rushing off to a dentist's appointment.

It was really only when I caught sight of the high grey walls and the rolling green sward with all the neat little markers that I fully realised where it was I was going. I stumbled off the bus, my long rust-coloured scarf that I always wear once the weather turns

autumnal nearly catching in the doors. I snatched it from the rubbery jaws just in time, the bus yielding it up with a dramatic sigh, and wound it several times around my neck, like some sort of comforting talisman, and then I headed through the big iron gates.

I couldn't find Mum's grave at first. We haven't been for ages, and anyway, we usually approach it from a different entrance because we take a different route in the car. For a few awful moments I thought I wasn't going to be able to find her among all these dead people, dead strangers, Byrnes and Campbells and O'Connors and Murphys and Langrells and Ryans and O'Hallorans and O'Dowds and Cogans and Hutchinsons. Dead people have all the same names as live ones. Well, obviously they must have, but still, it's sort of unexpected. I think it would be sensible if they arranged cemeteries alphabetically, like in a telephone book or a sort of gigantic *Who Was Who*, but I can see there would be practical difficulties. Still, it would make it much easier for visitors. As it is, it's like those supermarkets where they assume people are illiterate and don't alphabetise the fruit and vegetables at the weigh-point. (I know they think the people are illiterate, because they show helpful little pictures of the produce.)

Mum's grave had got sort of run in, you know, like a pair of shoes you've got used to. It doesn't have that sharp, pinched, forlorn, new look any more, and looking at it, almost middle-aged now in grave terms, I realised that by now there were other new girls and new boys, other families whose loss was more recent, and I felt almost envious of them, with their fresh, raw grief. The relatives of the people in the brown graves were still at the stage where people pressed their hands and murmured condolences, and their daughters and sons, if they had them, were probably still

not expected to turn in their homework with alacrity. Whereas my friends, my teachers, my neighbours have all got used to my not having a mother any more. But *I* haven't got used to it, and I don't see how I am going to get used to having a stepmother instead.

I felt a bit foolish then, standing by Mum's maturing, greening grave. I hadn't brought anything, flowers or that. I felt as if I'd made a social *faux pas*, like someone forgetting to bring grapes to a person in hospital. The sky was leaden, and although it was only lunchtime it felt like dusk. I tried to say a prayer, but that didn't work either. So in the end I just gave the wooden cross that is still on the grave a little pat, feeling very silly indeed but trying to show a bit of solidarity, and with an aching feeling in my throat, which is much worse than tears, I turned to go. As I went, a blackbird started singing from a chestnut tree. Most of the leaves had fallen from the tree, and it only took a minute or two to find the bird among the balding branches. I didn't know blackbirds sang in October, and I certainly don't know what he had to be so thrilled about on a cold grey afternoon like that, but there, that's nature for you. So much for the pathetic fallacy.

I arrived home as they were popping a champagne bottle in the drawing room. I don't think it was the first, actually. They were all a bit pink looking, and I don't think it was just the nip in the air. Still, I did my best not to look too ungracious, in spite of my jeans and woolly scarf, and I even drank half a glass, though I refused to clink glasses with Alva, who was over-excited because she'd never had a drink before. Instead I made a bit of a thing about holding Imelda's glass for her, which was maybe a bit disabledist of me, but at least it gave me something elaborate to do, and that is just what you need when you are feeling as awkward as I was feeling.

Fr Egan made a speech, which was really not at all the thing, in the circumstances, but I suppose the poor man was trying to make everything seem as normal as possible, which is daft – this is about as abnormal a situation as I can imagine. (OK, OK, if pressed I can imagine more abnormal situations, but not ones that are even remotely likely.) After that we all went around to the local *trattoria* for a plate of pasta. (We live in the sort of area where there *is* a *trattoria* around the corner. This is a far cry from Ballywhatsit and I hope that shower appreciate it.) Somebody must have tipped Luigi off (what are the odds on Fr Egan?) because he wheeled in a gigantic chocolate cake smothered in cream, to make it look more bridal, I suppose, with a plastic horseshoe on top and all lit up with birthday candles. It wasn't anyone's birthday, of course, but Luigi gets a bit over-enthusiastic. He isn't really Italian at all, but he pretends to be. He even has those awful circular neon lights in his restaurant that you only get in Italy, and he has a garish crucifix on the wall above the door into the kitchen, which isn't a door at all, but one of those ribbony curtains that you swish through.

The best thing that can be said about the whole affair is that the food was mega. Old Luigi might be a bit of a poser in his own way, but he knows how to cook.

Friday 24th October

After the wedding, I went to stay at Imelda's for a few days. That was my own idea. Tact, I suppose you could call it. Ashling and Alva went to stay somewhere too, leaving Dad and Margaret to get used to each other. At least, they're obviously well used to each other, but I suppose I mean to get used to being married to each other. They didn't go on a honeymoon. At least they spared

us all that embarrassment. So there they are, having their little honeymoon in our house. They didn't take any time off work, apart from the wedding day itself, but Dad said I needn't go back to school until next week. It must be funny Margaret going off to school every day from our house instead of me. Not funny ha-ha, of course, just funny peculiar. (That is an expression of Imelda's. I find it useful from time to time.) I wonder if people at school know yet. Some of the staff must know anyway. I can just imagine Gravyface going all wobbly in the neck at the idea, and as for Red Hugh, he'll be like a beetroot for a week. Iron Knickers will be very disapproving, but of course she won't be able to say so, which will kill her. I bet she'll try to arrange some sort of a little blessing ceremony, though, when she hears it was a registry office wedding. She'll find some tame Franciscan or something and create a liturgy, with candles and lots of movement and chanting from her little book of Taizé music. As long as she doesn't try to get the class involved.

I am going home tomorrow. Imelda said I could stay the weekend, but I think it would be better to go back there now and get acclimatised, so to speak, before school next week.

Saturday 25th October

Lisa's mother had her baby last night. It came early, nearly two months early, I think, and it's terribly tiny and in an incubator. Lisa rang me this morning, in a panic. She said they baptised it as soon as it was born. I said I was sure it would be all right, but she said she had been expecting a Sagittarian and now she'd got a Scorpio and she didn't think she could adjust so quickly. It's a girl, by the way, and they are going to call her Sandra. Well, I suppose they have already, if she's been baptised.

I was just coming in the hall door when the phone rang. Dad's car was in the drive, and Margaret's was parked at the kerb (Mum never had a car of her own), so I knew they were home, and I was steeling myself to say hello, but as soon as I put my key in the lock I could hear the phone bleating the way those new phones do. There is something very demanding about a ringing phone, so I tore into the house and picked it up at once, and it was Lisa with the news. She didn't ask where I'd been all week. She knew about the wedding, of course, but I didn't tell her the exact date. She probably doesn't even know yet that it's happened. I didn't tell her on the phone.

I found Dad and Margaret in the back garden. They obviously hadn't heard the phone. (I keep telling Dad we should reinstall the old phone, which gave a proper tring-tring. You can't hear the new one in the garden. But he likes new things, changes. I don't.) Margaret was harvesting the apples from a neighbour's old apple tree that overhangs our garden. I don't know if you are legally entitled to apples that grow on somebody else's tree even if they are technically in your garden, but anyway, the neighbours never pick even the ones on their side, so I suppose it's better not to waste them. She had a basket, one of those old-fashioned shopping baskets, and was laying the fruit carefully in it, one by one, layer by layer, and talking to Dad, who was raking up fallen leaves and rotting windfalls from around her feet. They looked like the very picture of domesticity, her with her ripe reddening apples and her little bulge, him with his rake, like one of those Dutch pictures of peasants doing peasanty things. It had an unreal quality about it.

Anyway I gave a little cough, because they evidently hadn't heard me, and Margaret put her basket down and came towards

me with her hand out, as if to shake mine, like a mayoress or somebody welcoming a visiting dignitary. Well, I didn't feel like being welcomed to my own home, so I pretended I didn't see the hand, but I managed a crooked sort of a smile, and I agreed to the coffee and barm (suck, swallow, sigh) brack she offered. Her hair looked worse than ever, all sort of flattened. I think it must be the kind of hair you need to use a ton of mousse on to give it shape. She didn't look the type to steal somebody's husband (OK, OK, widower). She looked extremely married, which of course she is, but it takes a lot of getting to used to that the person she is so extremely married to is my father. Sometimes I really hate him for this.

We all sat silently, awkwardly, around the kitchen table, drinking our coffee and eating our brack, which was delicious but I really only noticed that afterwards. At the time, it might as well have been compressed cottonwool. There was a new tablecloth on the table. We always had just an old PVC one. The new one is nice, chequered, sort of French-bistro looking, cheap and cheerful. But there was nothing wrong with the old PVC one. After a while, I noticed vague shadowy markings on the tablecloth, like those transfers you use to do embroidery, and I realised the old tablecloth was still there, underneath, its pattern showing lightly through. I found that comforting.

I told them about Lisa's mother's new baby. I was glad of something nice and neutral to talk about. Margaret was terribly interested, because of being pregnant I suppose. I even found myself telling her how Lisa was dismayed because the baby had the wrong birth sign, which made them both laugh. Dad laughed particularly loudly, gratefully, you might even think. I didn't look him in the eye. I couldn't.

Ashling and Alva arrived while we were eating. Ashling had her double-bass with her. I thought for a minute it was a coffin, when I saw her propping it up in the porch. It's twice as big as her. She had brought it on the bus. I wonder if she had to pay a fare for it? Their mum made a fresh pot of coffee. Alva was all excited about the brack – she's a terrible baby for fourteen – and she announced she wanted the biggest slice because it looked as if it must have the ring in it. Ashling said getting the ring didn't count unless it was actually Hallowe'en, which isn't for another week, and then Alva started to sulk, and her mother said there wasn't any ring in it, she'd come across it while she was cutting the brack and had damaged it so badly with the breadknife that she'd thrown it in the bin. Oh great, I thought, very auspicious, the first thing she does as 'mother' in this new family is throw a wedding ring in the bin. I know it's only the cheapest sort of metal, but that's not the point.

Sunday 26th October

Ashling and Alva are miffed because they have to share a room (them and the double-bass). They had their own rooms in their old house, except when somebody came to stay. Now they have the spare room. Very appropriate, I have to say. It's a lot smaller than my room, which is a source of satisfaction. At least nobody had the gall to ask me to move out of my bedroom. They have the spare room – I think I shall go on calling it that – all dickied out with ribbons and lace already. They both have mosquito nets over their beds. I told them we don't have mosquitoes in this part of Dublin, but they said they have them because they are 'pretty'. I was right about the Boyzone posters. They have one each, identical ones, stuck up over their beds, which I can't see the point of,

but I suppose if they had separate rooms before it may have made more sense.

When Margaret sells her house there will be some extra cash, and they are going to use it to do 'improvements' to this house. It doesn't need improving. It's perfectly all right. It's a very fine house. I hope Dad doesn't let Margaret redecorate it. I don't think I could live with the flowery things she is bound to want to put everywhere. I draw the line at primroses creeping up the dining room wall and sprigs of sweet pea dotted about the hall. The main plan is to open up the attic and put a new room up there for the girls, and then the baby can have the spare room. Alva is dead excited about it and sits around reading Velux brochures all the time, very childish. I hope they put another bathroom up there too, for their exclusive use. They are both for ever in the bath-room. You nearly have to make an appointment to go to the loo, never mind take a shower. It's going to be murder in the mornings, trying to get out to school on time.

Monday 27th October

I *knew* there'd be trouble over the bathroom this morning. A queue formed outside the bathroom door at about seven-thirty. It was like being in a youth hostel. I don't know which was worse, waiting in the queue or being inside the bathroom, knowing there was a queue outside. In future I am going to have my shower at night, and then all I'll have to do in the morning is beat the rush and use the loo. I can brush my teeth at the kitchen sink. I have already ensconced my toothbrush there, next to the cutlery drainer.

Margaret gave me a lift to school. I hadn't thought about that, but of course it doesn't make any sense my taking the bus while

she drives. It was the first time we'd been alone since this whole business started. In fact, it was the first time since that day of the counselling session. She gave me a cloth and asked me to clean the inside of the back window and to give the wing mirrors a wipe, as it was one of those fugged-up October mornings. Then I climbed into the front passenger seat and folded the cloth away in the glove compartment. At this point she was concentrating on pulling out into the traffic. It wasn't until we got to the first set of traffic lights that she had a minute to make conversation. I sat there, staring out of the front windscreen and hoping the lights would change quickly, so that there wouldn't be an opportunity to talk – Margaret is the sort of driver who needs all her concentration to drive – but those lights are very slow to change, as they are at a junction where a very insignificant road meets a major one with fast-flowing traffic, so of course they stayed red for ages, and, just as I feared, Margaret started to talk. It's funny, though, about cars. Sometimes it's easier to talk in a car, as you don't have to look the other person in the face. She put on her counselling voice, which is very low and concerned, and she said she knew the situation must be very awkward for me, and that she didn't for one moment think she could take the place of my (inhale, swallow, exhale) mother for me. I nearly choked. It hadn't even vaguely occurred to me that she might. I felt like snapping this at her. I knew she was trying to say the right thing, but sometimes the mere effort of someone trying to say the right thing is the very thing that makes what they say the wrong thing, the last thing you want to hear. With a major effort at self-control I said that I didn't want to talk about it if she didn't mind, that it had all happened now and we all just had to make the best of it. She flushed at that, but she didn't say any more, but that may have been because the

lights had changed and she needed to think about what she was doing. We didn't exchange another word till we got to the school gates, and then she said she would wait for me at four o'clock unless I had any extra-curricular activities. I'm in transition year, which means that everything is more or less extra-curricular for us, but I let that pass and I said I would meet her at the car at five past, thank you. I had thought fleetingly of making some excuse, so people wouldn't see me getting into her car, but I could see that they were all going to have to find out some time, so what was the point.

How right I was! The head nun announced the marriage at assembly, congratulating Mrs Ellis, as she called her. I nearly passed out. That's *Mum's* name. Lisa gave me a dig with her elbow and whispered: Jeez, Cindy, you never told me.

I hadn't seen her since the wedding, and I'd been too upset beforehand. A buzz was building up in the assembly hall. Everyone was saying that they'd been right she was pregnant, but god, Cindy Ellis's father! Some of them started to giggle, and I could feel the eyes of the whole school on me. It was dreadful. Then Margaret stood up, bright pink, and thanked everyone but she said she would prefer to go on being called Miss Magee. We always called her that, even though she should have been Mrs, I suppose. Maybe she didn't want people knowing she was married before. I can't see it being for feminist reasons. I felt better when she said that, though. I'm the only Ellis in this school, and I'd prefer if it stays that way. I'm glad Margaret doesn't want our name as well as everything else.

After assembly, everyone was fluttering around me, wanting to know about the wedding and everything. I said very quietly and firmly that I hadn't been at the wedding, and most people got the

message, I think, but one girl, Emma O'Mara in fifth year, who loves to gossip, persisted in asking her horrible, prurient, salacious questions – what did Milly-Molly-Mandy look like at breakfast, was she a good cook, what TV programmes does she watch, why had they not gone on honeymoon, did she sleep in my mother's bed? At that last question I let fly at her. I caught her by her horrible frizzy, wiry hair, a clump of it in each hand, and pulled like anything. She screamed and screamed, and Lisa hit me hard on the wrists to make me let go, and when I did Emma fell in a heap on the floor, weeping and clutching her head. Mr Gravy came along just then, and wanted to know what had happened. Everyone started to gabble at once, hysterically, but Lisa grabbed him by the elbow and pulled him aside and explained it all to him in a low voice. As soon as he heard what O'Mara had said, he took charge of the situation. He shooed all the others away, threatening them with detention if they were late for class, then he pulled her up off the floor and told her to stop snivelling and get to class at once. She went off, still moaning, lurching along by the wall, with her two hands to her head.

It has just occurred to me that the baby will be called Ellis too.

Monday 3rd November

Lisa's mother is out of hospital, but the baby is still in an incubator. She's doing really well, putting on weight and all, and she is out of intensive care, but she will be kept in hospital for a while yet. Lisa was telling me all this on Saturday. We went to Dunkin' Donuts, because we needed a treat, and we hadn't had a proper chat for ages. Lisa is worried about her mother. She said it is really time she stopped having babies and maybe it is time she thought about throwing her dad out. *Lisa!* I screeched. I mean, it's all very

76

well to give out about your parents, it's normal, but suggesting that your mum should throw your dad out, for no reason at all, that's going a bit far.

I was really shocked. But Lisa was adamant. She said they were always fighting, and she thought her mum just went on having babies to stop him from leaving, but that was a very bad reason to have babies. (Babies are a bad reason to get married, and keeping a marriage together is a bad reason for having babies — funny how babies and marriage are so mixed up.) She said that really they'd all be much better off without him. I couldn't believe my ears. I pointed out to her that they were the perfect family, all those lovely children, all those games of charades. Lisa stared. *Charades?* she said. We never play charades. Monopoly? I asked, Cluedo? Lisa said they never played anything, except when she played Happy Families with the little ones to keep them quiet on a Saturday afternoon while her father watched his football and drank himself silly (her expression) and her mother went to Crazy Prices. I said what about the division of labour between herself and her dad and taking it in turns to babysit on a Saturday? Huh! she sneered. He's the one that needs babysitting. All that going to parent–teacher meetings and coaching the school football team is just so much camouflage, she says.

I was flabbergasted. I had this vision of them all, but it seems it was all wrong. I must have made up the bit about the charades. Has your dad got a drink problem, Lisa? I asked, tentatively. A drink problem, she snorted. That's putting it mildly. He's just a raving alcoholic, a compulsive gambler and occasionally violent. Violent! I never knew. Oh Lisa! I said. And there I was complaining because my stepmother plays Neil Diamond at eight o'clock in the morning. Neil *Diamond* at eight o'clock in the *morning*, Lisa

screeched, full of indignation. Funny how even someone going through the sort of stuff she has to put up with can still sympathise about something pretty minor like that. Amazing sense of solidarity, really. (Of course, it's only minor by *comparison*. It doesn't feel a bit minor at the time. Not to mention Ashling and her wretched double-bass. It sounds like a very sick elephant.) And to think I was beginning to think Lisa wasn't being a good best friend. She's a star, really.

Lisa suspects the baby came early because of something her dad did, either that he'd actually knocked her mum about, or just that the strain of it all had got to her. I was sitting opposite her, and at this point I wriggled out of my seat and slipped around to the other side of the table and sat next to her. I put my arm around her shoulder and gave her a half-hug. She hugged me back, and we finished our doughnuts in silence. After that we went for a walk down Grafton Street, but we didn't do any window-shopping, like we usually do, we just walked along very close together, our shoulders almost touching and keeping in step with each other, just being friends. After that, Lisa had to go and do her babysitting bit.

Sunday 9th November

I'm not used to this sort of thing. I suppose with the Junior Cert and all, and Mum being ill, it's not been a madly sociable year for me. Nothing more thrilling than a school disco, held jointly with the only local boys' school the nuns approve of. (I don't know what criteria they use, but I suspect it may be the fact that it's a fee-paying school that swings it, even though ours isn't.) The problem with those things – apart from the absurd level of supervision – is that they make you dance with boys of your own age,

and we all know what fifteen-year-old boys are like – spotty, gauche, exceptionally immature, and obsessed with dirty jokes. And their feet smell. I think maybe all male feet smell, but it's worse at fifteen.

They seem to think that if you agree to dance with them, that's a licence to grope. You never get groped by anyone you wouldn't mind being groped by. That seems to be an immutable fact of life. And there is nothing worse than being groped by someone you don't want to be groped by. But you can't very well make a scene, or they'll call the whole thing off, and then nobody will get a chance to grope anyone, and I suppose on the law of averages, somebody somewhere must be getting some sort of a kick out of all this.

Anyway, that's all beside the point. I'm staying at Imelda's this weekend. Saturday was Ashling's seventeenth birthday, and they were having a party. I really didn't want to be there. For a start, I don't know any of her friends, and anyway I just couldn't bear the sort of party she wanted to have. They were all getting dressed up. Not fancy dress, I mean dressed up in ballgowns, all tulle and corsages. I mean, ballgowns are all very well if you're going to the Shelbourne in a taxi with a box of Leonidas chocolates and an orchid – and even then it's all a bit much – but at *home* (in this case, *my* home). I just couldn't face it, all those girls from their prissy school, with their partners in monkey suits. Ugh! And anyway, I haven't got anyone to be my partner. So I said I'd much rather spend the night with Imelda, and to tell the truth I think everyone was relieved. I think Ashling was afraid I'd stomp around in my Docs, stepping on people's toes and spitting into the fruit punch (mostly Aqua Libra and orange juice, with just enough cider to give it a whiff of alcohol, so they can pretend

they're being dead grownup). I wouldn't of course, but it's just as well that they should think I would.

Imelda and I went to hear some traditional music in the evening. I've never been into that stuff before, but this was good. It's different live, I suppose. I really enjoyed it, even though I was only drinking rock shandy. I wouldn't ask for a drink in a pub, it's not fair on the barman, and it would be mortifying to be refused, and anyway, I don't like beer.

We met these fellas with crash helmets. They were sitting across from us in the pub, and I think they were fascinated watching Imelda sipping her Guinness, which I held for her. Anyway, we all got chatting, and they were dead nice. I fancied one of them like mad, but I didn't think he was all that interested in me, just making conversation. But then at closing time we sort of strolled out of the pub together, the four of us, and they walked a little way with us, talking about this and that, joking together. They were really tickled that we were aunt and niece, and one of them – not the one I fancied, his mate – was being awfully gallant to Imelda, telling her we looked like sisters. I know he was just messing, but it was the first time I ever thought about us being similar, and when he came to mention it, I realised it was true. She is twice – no, nearly three times – my age, and she wears her hair really dead short so she doesn't have to worry about combing it, not even after she washes it, and mine is all long and tatty, but it's the same sort of murky brown and we have the same pale skin and dark eyes. Of course, I wear glasses most of the time and Imelda doesn't and she is small. I'm tall and still growing. Being around short people usually makes me uncomfortable, I feel as if I will break them if I touch them, but I don't feel like that with Imelda.

We came to our bus-stop and joined the queue. We had a long

wait, as we had missed the last ordinary bus and we had to wait for the midnight night-link. I had had a stone in my boot, so, since we had a long wait, I sat down on the pavement and undid my shoelaces. I eased the boot off, shook out the stone, and put the boot back on.

The two lads stood around, keeping us company till the bus came, joking me about the stone in my boot. One of them, the one who was playing up to Imelda, asked us to come on to a club with them. I was terrified Imelda was going to say yes, but she just threw her head back and laughed and laughed and asked them had they any idea what age she was. They said they were both twenty-two (which was probably an exaggeration), and that she was probably a year or two older. She shook her head and said that if they were twenty-two they were old enough to know better. She could easily have told them I was only fifteen, and far too young to be let into a nightclub (though I will be sixteen in three months), and even though I didn't want to go, I desperately didn't want her to say that either. But she didn't. Imelda never says anything embarrassing like that.

Then the bus came. We saw it at the end of the street, and I jumped up without lacing up my boot and started to get the fare out of my shoulder bag. I got the change ready, and was concentrating on making sure it was the right number bus – I always have to screw my eyes up – and flagging it down, and so I was completely thrown when Robbie, the younger of the two blokes, the better-looking one, the one I fancied, not the one who'd been making up to Imelda, put his hands heavily on my shoulders. I've never been mugged, but I thought they usually just grabbed your bag. I didn't think they would do a whole pick-up routine first.

My first instinct was to hug my bag really close to my body, pinioning it with my elbow and then I opened my mouth to scream, but before I got properly started, Robbie was kissing me, hotly and hurriedly, a bus-stop sort of kiss. Because my mouth was already open, I could feel his breath right down into my throat, and his tongue briefly brushed my upper teeth. Then he pulled away and pushed me gently towards the bus, which Imelda had already boarded.

She was struggling with her purse, blocking the doorway. I stumbled up the steps, anxious to help her, but by this time she had got herself sorted out and paid my fare. As soon as he'd got the money, the driver simultaneously started the bus and closed the doors, though I was still hanging onto the central bar and standing in the well of the doorway. I must have still had one foot on the pavement, because I can remember that I jerked it up really quickly when I realised that the doors were about to close, but I wasn't quick enough, because my foot got stuck between the doors, the foot with the unlaced boot.

I yelled at the driver to open the doors, that my foot was caught, but I was giggling and struggling, and I think he thought I was messing. Maybe he thought I'd been drinking. Anyway, he ignored me at first and hung out of his side window, watching for his chance to pull into the flow of traffic. I kicked and struggled a bit more, still yelling at him to open the doors. I yanked really hard and my foot shot out of my boot, but just at that moment the driver must have realised I was serious, because just as I shot forward, released from my boot, the doors opened and the boot fell out and clunked onto the road. At that very moment, the driver saw an opportunity and he pulled out from the bus stop and sped off into the night, leaving me giggling and heaving in a clump on

the floor, and my lovely new (well, newish) Doc Marten lying in the roadway.

I didn't dare yell at him to stop the bus, and anyway, I was giggling so much I couldn't have got it out even if I'd tried. Get up, you eejit you, said Imelda, toeing me in the ribs, and I struggled to my feet, and limped down the bus behind her, one shoe off and the other shoe on, like Diddle-Diddle-Dumpling, my-son-John. The pair of us collapsed into a seat, and it was only then that Imelda realised I'd lost my footwear.

She wanted to go and tell the driver to stop, but by this stage we were a good quarter of a mile from the bus-stop, and it was too late. The driver might stop, but he wasn't going to wait for me to hop back a quarter of a mile, pick up my boot and put it on, and then run to catch up, and the next bus wouldn't be until one o'clock. So we sat tight, swaying with the onward rush of the bus, which was travelling far too fast, and lurching against each other, occasionally getting another gale of giggles at the memory of what had happened.

At one point, after we had sobered up a bit, I lifted up my stockinged foot and wiggled my toes, and that started the pair of us off again. I'm sure the driver thought we were paralytic.

Just as the bus careered around a corner we heard a horn being tooted in a doodle-de-doo-doo rhythm and I pressed my face up against the window of the bus, making a peephole around it with my hands, just in time to see a motorcycle with two people on it zooming along the road we were turning off, almost grazing the side of the bus with the speed of it. I couldn't be sure, I could only see two helmets and two figures, but I think it was Robbie and Ger, and I fancy I saw the one on the pillion trailing something in the wind behind him, something clumpy and dangling on what

might have been a bootlace. They whizzed by with a roar, and anyway the bus was just leaning off into a side road as the bike whipped along, but I could have sworn I heard a laugh riding on the afterbreeze of the motorbike.

We went straight to bed when we got back to Imelda's. At least, Imelda went to bed, and I pulled out the 'put-you-up', as Imelda jokingly calls it – she always says this with a middle-England rural sort of accent, I don't know why – which is cleverly tucked away in the sofa, and made up my makeshift bed. The duvet and things are kept in a plain wooden chest under the window. It doubles as a sort of primitive window seat.

I was glad we didn't stay up to chat and make hot chocolate. I was happy to slip under the duvet and lie in the dark, savouring the memory of my first kiss – hardly a memory, it still seemed almost to be present in my body fibres, in spite of all the jostling and giggling since it had happened. I lay there in the dark and replayed the scene in my head, like a video, and I smiled at myself for thinking he was trying to mug me.

Monday 10th November

I woke up with a smile on my face still, though I couldn't remember why. And then I remembered the kiss. Fifteen is probably a bit old for a first kiss nowadays, I realise that, but it wasn't technically a first kiss. There was that awful time when I was thirteen and my cousin organised something for me. She was going out with her boyfriend – she was fourteen – but of course she couldn't tell them at home that she was, as they wouldn't let her out with a boy. (They still won't, even though she's sixteen now.) So she had to pretend she was going to the cinema with me. I was delighted. We were staying with her family at the time,

on holiday, and it was pretty boring, so a night out at the cinema seemed like a great treat to me. But as soon as we were out the gate she announced she was really going to meet Ed and they were going to go into the woods. I shrugged and said I would go to the cinema anyway. That wouldn't be necessary, she said. She had me fixed up with Alan. I was shocked and excited at the same time. Alan was very goodlooking and desirable and I had been admiring him from a distance for some time, but I'd had no idea Marianne knew this. I said OK and tagged along, brimming with anticipation, to the meeting place, which was near the entrance to the woods. (It wasn't really a wood, it was just a little plantation of trees, maybe ten yards by four.) Anyway, to cut a long story short, it turned out not to be Alan at all. It was somebody else, his name was Alan, but he wasn't the Alan I'd had in mind, he was much older, seventeen, which to a thirteen-year-old is like a grown-up, and he wore these grey trousers, real trousers, not jeans, and a tie, and I was terrified of him. When he tried to kiss me, I felt my whole body stiffen and go rigid in his arms, and I remember that I kept my own arms dead straight against my sides and I curled my lips in between my teeth, so that you couldn't see any mouth, just a gash across my lower face. Still, he tried to kiss me, a horrible sloppy, wet, warm kiss, like a dog's lick.

The worst part of the whole experience was the embarrassment. I couldn't explain to him why I was so shocked to see him, I couldn't tell him I had been expecting a younger and more handsome Alan. It was awful, really, really awful, and I was sure he would think I was frigid. I didn't really know what that meant (I still don't), but I knew from reading magazines that it was not the thing to be.

That was technically my first kiss, but I don't count it. I don't

count the snatched slobberings at school discos either. I count Robbie, though, because, even though it was a snatched kiss too, and completely unexpected, it was totally and utterly delicious.

Wednesday 12th November

I wonder if I will ever see Robbie again. I think it's probably more romantic if I don't. The whole thing has a sort of perfection about it as it is, ships that pass in the night, a fleeting kiss, a moment of intimacy, and then no more. Mad!

But maybe romance isn't what I want. I think maybe that's true. It's not romance I want, it's *a* romance, which is quite different. A real flesh-and-blood boyfriend is probably worth quite a lot of fleeting kisses at bus-stops. And he is lovely. Oh well. I suppose a fleeting kiss at a bus-stop is better than nothing. Or maybe it's not. Maybe it's worse than nothing. It has had a very unsettling effect. I keep thinking I see him in the street, and then the person turns around and it's somebody else entirely. I can't really keep his face in my mind, if I'm honest, but I think I would know it if I saw it all the same. His eyes turn up at the corners.

Monday 17th November

Lisa's little sister was christened yesterday. At least, she was baptised ages ago, when she was born, so they just had a little ceremony for family and friends at the house yesterday, to make up for not having a proper christening, and we were all invited, me and Dad and Margaret and Ashling and Alva.

We never went anywhere before all together like that, like a real family. It felt kind of weird, all piling into the car. Margaret got to sit in the front passenger seat, beside Dad, who drove, of

course, because that is the sort of family this is, and anyway Margaret is a very nervous driver, and Ashling and Alva and I sat in the back, in a row. Ashling and I made Alva sit in the middle, on the hump, because she is the youngest and also the smallest, but mainly because she is the youngest, and we had the two door places. It was very cramped, but only Alva moaned about it. Ashling and I were very mature and we made long-suffering faces at each other over the top of Alva's head. I had never exchanged a meaningful look with Ashling before. Ashling isn't too bad really, it's Alva that is the real pain.

She saved me some birthday cake from her party last week, icecream cake it was, and gave it to me on Sunday evening when I came home. It was quite funny really, I arrived in a pair of Imelda's slippers, which were the only things of hers I could get my feet into (she's smaller than me). Luckily it was a dry day, because I think the soles of those things are only made of cardboard and they would probably have disintegrated in the rain. I couldn't find my key, so there I was standing in the porch, slapping my pockets, when Ashling saw my shadow through the glass and let me in. She stepped backwards into the hall when she saw these two daft things on my feet — they are sort of novelty slippers that somebody with very poor taste gave Imelda for Christmas one year, and they are in the shape of dalmatians' heads. I had brought my other Doc home with me, because I couldn't bear to throw it in the bin, but I didn't have room for it in the little bag I had, so I was carrying it under my arm. I must have looked very peculiar, because Ashling started to smile, but she is too polite to guffaw out loud (which is what I would have done). Seeing the little smile on her face, I began to see the funny side, and I found myself telling her the whole story, down to the

two fellas at the bus-stop, though I didn't mention the kiss, I thought that was private. I am not sure if even Imelda knows about that. Either she was too busy fumbling for change for the bus, or she is very tactful, because she didn't say a word. I think she genuinely didn't see it. I hope so, because even though I am very fond of Imelda, I love the idea of me and Robbie being the only two people in the whole world who know about that kiss. We are the only two who know what it felt like anyway.

We all arrived at Lisa's house a bit creased and squashed. I was back in my brown school shoes (I haven't had the courage yet to tell Dad about losing one of my boots) with one of Ashling's kilts, because my jeans got torn in the incident on the bus too, which I didn't discover until the next morning, and it was too cold for one of my Lisbon dresses, and the only other thing I had was my school uniform or Mum's tracksuit, neither of which was suitable for the occasion. I am going to have to get some more things to wear, but I hate spending money on clothes, as I am growing all the time at the moment, so it seems a bad investment. I have an economical streak. I think I get that from Dad. The kilt was a bit prissy on me, even though it is a short one, but it does a nice little swing when you walk, which I think is the effect of the pleating. I wouldn't mind getting a skirt for Christmas.

The christening was lovely. Fr Egan was there, and he blessed the baby (who is home now, and very, very tiny, but doing fine), and formally named her Sandra even though he couldn't rechristen her, and there was champagne and little lumps of paté on soggy Ritz biscuits and cocktail sticks with cubes of cheddar and glacé cherries and grapes and olives skewered onto them. I can't think why people do that. The combination of glacé cherries and cheese is revolting. Afterwards, we had christening cake and

coffee. Alva wanted to have champagne, but her mother wouldn't let her and she wailed, But I *always* have champagne, I *love* it. Which is of course a complete exaggeration. It just goes to show that if you let a kid like that have an inch she'll take a mile.

Lisa's mother was dead proud of Sandra, and she walked around talking to all the guests with her all wrapped up in a little pink blanket. I think pink is putrid, especially when it is used to colour-code babies. The poor little creature is very red and her skin is a size too big, so that she looks like a scalded tomato, so all in all the shocking pink they make her wear doesn't exactly suit her, but even so, you couldn't help admiring the tiny little fingers, the way they curl around your finger, and sort of wave and wriggle, each one individually, as if they were alive, I mean alive in their own right. She has lots of hair, jet black, but it's sort of glued together in places with cradle-cap (baby-crap Lisa calls it, which is a bit crude), and the wrinkles in the palms of her hands are really deep. She makes the most tremendous racket when she cries, like a smoke alarm. You wouldn't believe a thing so small could make so much noise – though come to think of it, smoke alarms aren't very big either – and she really throws her whole body into it. She looks like a prisoner trying to escape when you see the blanket heaving and churning with her all wrapped up inside it. The funny thing is, when that smoke alarm goes off, the one thing you want to do is stop the dreadful, penetrating noise it makes, but you don't want to stop it just because it assaults your eardrums, you want to stop it because she really convinces you when she does it that she is in some sort of a serious predicament, and urgently needs adult attention.

Sandra's mother thrust her at me at one point in the proceedings, as I was the nearest person without a drink in my hand when

the doorbell went. I think she didn't want to take the baby out to the hall, as she is so tiny, and it's draughty out there. They have to be extra careful with her. She weighed hardly anything, like a kitten in a nightdress, and she started to mewl in my arms – not her smoke alarm imitation, just sort of unhappy squeaks and squawks. Margaret came rushing over to me. I could see she was bursting to take Sandra from me, and she had the silliest smile on her face. I think she must be in the mushy stage. Anyway, she didn't take the baby from me, but she showed me how to hoist her up on my shoulder and walk her around, giving her little rhythmic pats on the back. It was sort of sweet really. I suppose it reminded her in advance, if you see what I mean, of her own baby. It worked. Sandra stopped mewling and started making the softest little purring sounds you ever heard. Maybe she really is a sort of kitten baby.

I had meant to keep a lookout for signs of dysfunctionality in Lisa's parents' marriage, but what with minding the baby and everything, I forgot all about it. I'm not sure what I expected to see anyway. The whole thing about the way they behave is that they present this façade of happiness and togetherness, and I don't suppose there would be mounds of gin bottles in the back garden or anything like that. Sometimes I wonder if Lisa is not just making it all up, to get attention, but then I feel ashamed of thinking like that. Nobody really knows what goes on in other people's families. Although what goes on in my family is all fairly public. A bit too public, for my taste – it is no fun knowing that the whole school knows your father knocked up one of the teachers and they had to get married, not to mention the indecent haste with which all this happened after your mother died. Still, I suppose those things are a bit of a nine days' wonder, and I don't

hear all that much about it now, though they probably say things behind my back. I think old Gravyface giving Emma O'Mara a piece of his mind was a help. She keeps well out of my way anyway, thank the stars.

Thursday 20th November

There was a mysterious message on the fridge for me when I got home from school today. Margaret is one of these neurotically tidy people, and she has all these systems going. It's quite nice to have a tidy house, but the systems drive me mad. I feel like sabotaging them sometimes, but then I catch sight of her sort of lugging herself around and I feel sorry for her. She's a bit long in the tooth for coping with the stresses of a pregnancy, and I don't suppose it would be very fair to start making things difficult for her. I can be a very tolerant and thoughtful person, although most people don't seem to appreciate this.

Anyway, one of these systems of hers has to do with phone messages. She has a little sticky pad by the phone in the hall, and by the one in their bedroom too, I think, and when anyone rings up for someone who is not there, whoever takes the call is supposed to write the message on one of the sticky slips and put it on the fridge. She has little magnets on the fridge too. They are not for holding the messages, as those are self-sticking. Instead, they are for dividing up the fridge door into areas. Each magnet is in the shape of a letter, and your initial is supposed to indicate your area, and all your messages are supposed to be left in the area under your initial. You have to sort of imagine that the fridge is divided up into columns, and each column is headed by a letter, all in alphabetical order of course (maybe Margaret could get a job advising graveyards about how to sort out their occupants).

Ashling and Alva have the same initial, but they are in different colours. The only thing is, I can never remember which one is which, so if I have a message for either of them, I just leave it sort of hovering between their two columns. I think this irritates Margaret intensely, but she is working hard at not showing her irritation. I wish she would. A good fight would be great to clear the air. It gets a bit tense around here, with everyone being so nice to everyone else. Even Dad is on his best behaviour. It can't go on like this. I mean, this is supposed to be a family, a home, but it's like being on permanent guest terms with everyone else. It's not clear who are the hosts and who are the guests in this situation, but I think that's because we are all both at different times, or maybe even at the same time. It's tricky.

Anyway, there was this message for me, under my C magnet. I don't know who took it. I can't distinguish their handwritings yet. It just said a Dr Martin phoned for me, and left a number. Our doctor is called Marron. I wondered if somebody had mis-heard the name, but we are on very friendly terms with our doctor, after Mum's illness, and if she did need to ring up, which I can't imagine she would, she wouldn't leave a message that Dr Marron rang, she'd say Nuala rang, and anyway, it wasn't her number, because I checked in the book.

I decided I wasn't going to ring the number that had been left, until I had thought about it a bit more. I suppose it could be the PhD sort of doctor – we have one or two of those at school, but none of them is called Martin. I suppose the Martin could be a christian name?

Friday 21st November

Another message on the fridge. This time, it said that Dr Martin was trying to get in touch with me about a 'podiatric' appointment. (Somebody can't spell.) I began to get a bit concerned at this. Paediatrics has to do with babies and children. Is someone trying to be smart? Or is there some sort of mixup? Maybe it's really for Margaret, something to do with the baby. Maybe I should just ring up the number and see. Or maybe there is something unpleasant going on here. I think I'll try ringing the number, but I'll ask Lisa to be with me when I do, in case it is some sort of pervert.

Saturday 22nd November

I went over to Lisa's with the sticky slips from the fridge this morning. She is pretty sharp, and she always knows what area of the city a phone is in by the number. I'm hopeless at that sort of thing.

I found Lisa feeding the baby. Her mother couldn't manage breastfeeding with all the other children to attend to, as it would have meant going in and out to the hospital all the time. She needed to be fed every two hours in the beginning. That's why she's on the bottle, even though she is still so young.

I told Lisa the story, and she was as puzzled as I was when I said some doctor had been ringing for me. To tell the truth, I had been beginning to get a bit worried. Maybe it wasn't a hoax after all. Maybe it was some clinic, ringing to tell me I had something wrong with me. I had a blood test once when I had a bad bout of 'flu and they wanted to be sure it wasn't some mystery virus. I don't remember ever getting the results. That was six months ago, but maybe they lost the sample and it's just turned up.

Anyway, when Lisa saw the second slip, she said, It's not paediatric, you dolt, it's podiatric. I know, I said, that must be just a spelling mistake. But apparently it wasn't. I'm supposed to be the one who is good at English, but I didn't know that there is a branch of medicine called podiatrics. Apparently it's a sort of upmarket word for chiropody. Well, that wasn't much help. I don't have corns or bunions or an ingrown toenail, and I don't suppose they would show up in a blood test anyway. Verrucas might, though.

What was the doctor's name again? asked Lisa, burping the baby. Martin, I said, Dr Martin. It was only when I said it aloud that it hit me. It hit Lisa too at the same moment. Doc Marten. Doc Marten boots! It had to be somebody who knew something about my lost boot. Oh my god, I thought, it's Robbie. I started to shake. My heart started to thump wildly against my rib cage as if it wanted to get out of my body. My tongue grew an instant covering, like the sort of cover you can buy to put on a hot water bottle, thick and furry and dry.

I don't know why I jumped to the conclusion that it was Robbie. It could have been Imelda, for example. She might have been playing a joke. I snatched the slip of yellow paper from Lisa, and examined the number again. No, it wasn't Imelda's number, and I was pretty sure it wasn't her office number either. I don't know her office number offhand, but I'd recognise it if I saw it. It might have been the bus-driver. No, it couldn't possibly be the bus-driver. He didn't know my name, he didn't even know I'd lost my shoe. It might have been Robbie's friend. What's his name? Gerry, Gerard, something like that. Just Ger, I think, yes, Ger. But how could it be Robbie anyway? He didn't know my name any more than the bus-driver did. No, no, he did, he knew

my first name. Well, that wouldn't be much help, he wouldn't be able to find me in the phone book under my first name.

This looks like a lot of thinking on paper, but it only took me seconds to think it in my head, even with my heart leaping about in my chest and my fingers shaking. As I stood there, gaping at the phone number, I became vaguely aware that Lisa was saying something. It was like hearing somebody far away, on the other side of something big and soft, like a cottonwool mountain. What? I said. What? What?

I *said*, repeated Lisa with exaggerated patience, laying the baby back in her crib – she had nodded off at this stage, and she looked perfectly sweet, her little eyelids all pale and blue-lined and her face puckered and relaxed at the same time. Babies are OK. I *said*, What does the phone number begin with?

Four, I said, it starts with four. Four what? Four nine, I said, Four nine two. That's a local number, she mused. Well, I should have known that. I mean, that's what our number starts with, that's what Lisa's starts with too, but I wasn't thinking very clearly.

I realised Lisa didn't know about Robbie. She'd heard the story about the Doc getting stuck in the bus doors. The whole class had heard that and we'd all had a good laugh about it. I'd been a minor celebrity on the strength of it for a good two days, class clown, that's me, if I'm not fainting in algebra I'm beating up a fifth year or entertaining the masses with tales of my weekend adventures. Lisa'd made the connection all right, as soon as I said Dr Marten out loud, but she didn't know about Robbie. So I told her. Oh my god, she said. He *kissed* you. And you'd never even *met* him before. Oh lord!

I hadn't told the story properly, obviously. I'd only told her the

facts. She was seeing it as the next thing to rape, whereas it wasn't like that at all, it was completely different. I hadn't made her understand what it was like, that it was a gentle kiss, a sweet kiss, a loving kiss, a thrilling kiss, not ugly, not slobbery, not rough. A kiss can be a surprise and still not be an intrusion. It took a while to convince her, but when I did, she started to get all enthusiastic.

Well, you'll have to ring him, she said. He's rung you twice, after all. He must be keen. My heart, which had calmed down a bit by now, started off again, at an even faster pace this time. Oh lord, I thought, if this is what love is like, I think I'd rather pass on it, there's just too much stress involved. And suddenly I thought of Dad and his phonecalls to and from Margaret in the early days of their relationship, and I wondered if their hearts had raced like this too. I felt a moment of tenderness for the two of them, ringing each other up, furtively, nervously, uneasily, those first few times at least.

Come on, said Lisa firmly. Let's ring this podiatrician. Ask him does he do left shoes only.

So I did. I rang the number, and a woman answered. I slammed the phone down immediately I heard her voice.

Cop yourself on, said Lisa. It's probably his mother.

His mother?

Yes, he probably has a mother. Most people do. Oops, sorry, Cindy.

She squeezed my arm when she said that. I didn't mind. I know she wasn't being cruel. But still, I felt the tears starting in my eyes. I swallowed and thought about chocolate cake. That's a little trick I've learned.

I rang again. The woman answered again, her voice sharp, probably anticipating another slamdown. I... I... I'm sorry, I seem

to have been cut off the last time, I started. The thing is, I don't know if I have the right number, but I'm looking for...

And then I stopped dead. I couldn't tell his mother I was looking for a Dr Martin. She'd tell me I had a wrong number and hang up. Lisa snatched the phone from me. My tongue had grown its hot-water bottle cover again, and I couldn't go on. ...a friend, she said. His name is Robbie, she went on, bright and clear. I don't know his second name, I'm afraid, but he gave me this number.

Then she stopped talking. There was silence for several seconds. I couldn't bear to ask her what was happening, when suddenly she thrust the phone at me, jamming it up against my ear, It's him, she hissed, it's Robbie.

I swallowed the hot-water bottle cover and said, Hello?

Hello? he said back.

I recognised the voice at once.

Oh, Robbie, it's you, I said. I was afraid it might be Dr Martin.

He laughed, and I was grinning so widely my face hurt. Lisa tiptoed away, a delighted grin on her face too. She needn't have. We didn't say much, but we arranged that he would call around tomorrow, to deliver my boot.

Sunday 23rd November

I think this has been the happiest day of my life. At least, the second half of it was happy. The morning was sheer agony, waiting for Robbie to come. I didn't know whether I wanted him to come or not. Half of the time, I was afraid he wouldn't turn up, and the other half of the time I was afraid he would.

We had made an arrangement for three o'clock. I couldn't eat my lunch. Dad was all concern. He made me some tea and tucked me up with a rug on the sofa. My fingers were stiff with cold as I

took the cup from him, and I could hardly move my feet, they had seized up. Dad decided I was coming down with flu and he lit a fire for me. I couldn't tell him the truth. Nerves always make me cold. But anyway, I think he likes me to be sick. It gives him an excuse to be fatherly. Sometimes I think he finds it difficult, and I know he's feeling dead guilty. Not that I would ever let him know I know. He deserves to feel guilty.

Three o'clock came and went. No Robbie. He's lost the address, I decided. Three-oh-five, he's changed his mind. Three-ten, he's met somebody else. Ashling was practising. I could hear the elephant moaning from her bedroom.

At a quarter past three the front doorbell rang. The elephant stopped moaning. I'll get it, called Ashling, glad of a chance to take a break, I'd say. I don't know how she stands that noise. It's like one of those jungle vet programmes they have on the television. It'll be the milkman, I said to myself. It wasn't the milkman – it couldn't be, on a Sunday – it was the woman next door wanting to borrow a ladder. Ashling got it for her. I heard her dragging it around the side of the house. I bet the woman next door only wanted to get a look at the new stepfamily. She's an awful old wagon really. I'm sure she was disappointed in Ashling, she's so neatly dressed and well-behaved, like a doctor's receptionist. Then Ashling came back in through the front door, and then the kitchen door slammed. The elephant started moaning again before too long.

At twenty-five past three I thought I heard a knock, and then the doorbell rang again. I bet the woman next door doesn't know how to extend the ladder, I thought. This time she's hoping Margaret will answer.

But it wasn't that. It was Robbie. It was Alva who answered the

door. I could hear her silly little girl's voice in the hall. Cindy, she called out. You're wanted at the door. And then I could hear her thumping up the stairs. I didn't know why she ran away like that. She usually hangs around to see what's going on.

The front door hadn't been closed. My god, she left him standing on the doorstep. I threw the rug off and struggled to my feet. I don't why it was such a struggle. I suppose I'd got sort of stuck in the role of invalid. As I went out into the hall, I could hear voices from the kitchen, somebody was singing softly, and there was a clatter of dishes.

Robbie, I said, though I couldn't actually see the person at the door, only a shape against the slanting wintry sun. It must have been a full second after I'd said his name that I realised I *hadn't* actually said it. My lips and tongue had made the right shapes, but my vocal chords must have been asleep. I coughed, to wake them up, and said, Come in.

When he stepped into the hall, I knew for sure it was he. I still couldn't see his face clearly, but I just knew by the way he stood next to me, by the bulk of his body, his stance, the way he put his head down, and finally, by the way he kissed me again, lightly but urgently, softly but deeply, there in my own hallway, with my stepsisters upstairs and my stepmother singing 'Sweet Caroline' in the kitchen and the dishwater gurgling down the drain. This time, I wasn't taken by surprise. This time, I kissed him back.

Sorry I'm so late, he said. Couldn't find the house.

It turned out he'd got my number from Imelda. He and Ger had followed the bus that night, at a distance, intending to watch for us getting off, and then to give me back the boot and say good night. But the bus veered off suddenly down a side road, at one point, and they didn't have time to signal, so Ger kept going

straight on, though he tooted the horn. By the time they'd managed to make a U-turn and come after us again, our bus had disappeared. They'd cruised around for a while, hoping to catch it again, but they couldn't find it, so they'd chucked it in for that night. But Robbie said he couldn't stop thinking about me (well, naturally), and besides, he said, it was a perfectly good boot, a shame to waste it, so, as he put it, he started doing a bit of research. He found out what the bus-route was, and he walked along it a few times, hoping to catch sight of me. And one day he spotted Imelda coming home from work, and he hailed her and told her he had my boot, and that he wanted to return it.

Imelda offered to return it for him (the mean thing), so he was driven to explain that actually the boot was only an excuse, he really wanted to see me again. So then Imelda interviewed him extensively – and by the way established that he is only eighteen, not twenty-two as Ger had claimed – before she entrusted him with my number, but she did give it to him in the end, which means she must have decided he was OK, and she agreed not to tell me. He wanted to surprise me. I found all this out afterwards. He didn't tell me the whole story there in the hall, of course, but he did just mention that he'd brought the boot.

Well, then, where is it? I asked.

Where's what?

The Doc. The boot. What you came to deliver.

Oh that, he said, and he looked sheepish. Alva took it, he said. I explained to her why I was here, and she snatched it out of my hand and ran up the stairs with it, to show it to A... her sister.

What did Alva want with my boot? I wondered. Maybe she was playing a joke of some sort. Not a very funny joke. And how come Robbie knew her name?

You must have introduced yourself to Alva, then, I said.

What? Oh yes, yes, I did. I didn't know she lived here.

Why did he say that? I wonder. An odd sort of comment to make. Maybe he meant he didn't know I had sisters.

She's not my real sister, I said hastily.

No, of course not, he said, as if he knew all about our family history, though of course he couldn't. Not even Alva could explain all that in the half-minute she had spent at the front door.

Robbie didn't leave until after five. Dad came up from the kitchen with some tea, and I introduced Robbie. I said he was a friend that I'd met through Imelda, which was only half-untrue. The others came in then too, for tea, Alva swinging my boot by its lace.

Yours, I believe, Cindy, she said, with a hand on her hip, still swinging the boot, tantalisingly.

Give it to me! I cried, reaching for it, pretending to join in the fun, but really I was a bit annoyed at her for trying to steal the limelight. This playing around with the boot was only to attract attention.

I tried it on, Alva went on, and so did Ashling. But it didn't fit either of us. Way too big for our dainty little feet, wasn't it, Ash?

Give her the boot, Alva, said Ashling, blushing madly. I can't imagine why.

So then Alva relented and tossed the boot at me. She threw it quite hard. I think she hoped it would hurt, but I caught it, so it didn't.

Thanks, I said, through gritted teeth, wishing they would all go away again, and leave me alone with Robbie. But Margaret had started into conversation with him, and Alva kept hovering around him and darting into the conversation whenever she could. I don't

think she was really doing it to annoy me, just trying to get Robbie's attention.

We all had tea then. Dad poured. It was just like in those books about how to bring up your teenagers, making their friends welcome in the house, but it didn't feel a bit priggish or prissy or anything, it was just nice, fine, right, and Robbie was really polite to everyone, though I noticed he blushed like mad when he was introduced to Ashling and seemed to avoid eye contact with her all afternoon. But he behaved so well, I could have kissed him. (Well, I did, oh yummy.) He talked to Alva about some singer she is into (the 90s equivalent of Neil Diamond, no doubt) and told her about someone he knows who can get her tickets for a gig he is doing in the Point next month. Alva seemed really excitable. I don't think it was just about the tickets. I think she fancied Robbie, actually.

And he talked to Dad about motorbikes, which I didn't even know Dad was interested in, and to Margaret about how to make apple jelly. I don't know how they got onto that one, but it turns out that Robbie's dad is majorly into gardening and Robbie and his mum are at their wits' end trying to use up all the fruit and vegetables he produces. Robbie knows all about blanching beans for the freezer and where to get Kilner jars reasonably. I never even heard of Kilner jars.

It sounds really stupid, but it wasn't, it was just nice and normal. I haven't felt so normal for a long time. I wasn't even embarrassed by my family. I'd prefer if Margaret didn't lurch quite so pregnantly, and there are all sorts of things wrong with it as a family, not least that Mum isn't in it, but when you come to think about it, it's as good a family as lots of people's – better than Lisa's lovely idyllic one anyway, by all accounts. I didn't explain it all to him.

I will of course, but not just yet.

Ashling was very quiet. I wonder if she is not feeling too well. She just sat there, looking at the carpet. She didn't even have any tea. But Alva kept gaping at Robbie and offering him shortbread biscuits. She said afterwards he was absolutely gorgeous and she wished she had a boyfriend like him. (I knew all along she fancied him.) He's not my boyfriend, I said. Well, who is he then? she asked. He's..., I started, oh, well, yes, I suppose he is sort of my boyfriend. I didn't even blush when I said it. And it must be sort of true, because as he was leaving he asked if he could see me again, and I said I'd ring him. I'd rather leave it like that for the moment, just till I get used to the idea. I've never been on a proper date before, and I want to think about it first.

Tuesday 25th November

Lisa is dying to meet Robbie, and I am under strict instructions to bring him around to her house. She can't go out much at the moment, because of having to help to mind the baby. I really must make a point of going to see her more often. I mean, I see plenty of her at school, but she must be feeling isolated outside of school hours, and anyway, I need to get practice in with newborn babies. It's only three more months.

Thursday 27th November

It's finally happened, we've had a row. It didn't work at all. I thought it might clear the air, but it only made things worse, I think.

It started with me and Alva. She borrowed my Docs, the famous Doc Martens that brought me and Robbie together – not very

romantic, objectively speaking, and yet extremely romantic in a funny sort of way. But the thing is, she didn't ask. She just took them. Not that I would have let her have them, even if she had asked. I mean, there are things you don't lend. I wouldn't mind lending her a cardigan or even a hairband, but I wouldn't let anyone else wear my shoes.

I suppose in a way it was kind of touching that she did want to borrow them, a sort of a tribute. She copies Ashling in everything, wears exactly the same sort of clothes as she does, reads her books, I mean, even the twin Boyzone posters are an indication of how much she is in her sister's shadow. I used to think that was Margaret's fault, that she went around dressing them up like twins, and maybe she did when they were younger, but now that I know them better, I just think Alva is a natural follower, and Ashling has been the obvious one to follow. Now there's me, though. It never even occurred to me that she might want to copy me, but then I've never had a little sister before. Not that I think of her as a sister. As far as I am concerned, Ashling and Alva are just two boring girls who live in this house too.

Anyway, to get back to the story about the Docs. I came home from school yesterday and went upstairs as usual to my room to change out of the dreaded uniform. I had got into my black gear, but I couldn't find my boots anywhere. I groped about under the bed and I looked under the chair, in the bottom of the wardrobe, and even in the fireplace – it's disused, so I sometimes pitch shoes in there. No boots. I am careless with things, so it didn't occur to me that somebody had taken them, I just assumed I'd left them somewhere stupid. Sometimes I take them off when I am watching TV if I want to put my feet up. Not even I am a big enough slob to plonk my Docs on the sofa. It is Mum's sofa after all, and

is due a bit of respect. She was very houseproud. I think I said that before.

I took no notice of the missing boots, just put on a pair of slippers, and went off and did my homework. But when I was going to bed, there they were, lined up neatly under my bed. I knew they hadn't been there earlier. The only explanation was that somebody had put them there in the meantime. I still didn't think much of it. I assumed Margaret had found them somewhere about the house and had kindly put them in my room. Actually, no, it wouldn't really be a kindness, it would be a compulsion. She wouldn't put them in my room so that I would find them, she would put them there because she couldn't bear them to be anywhere else. But that is an academic point, because it wasn't Margaret, as I found out when I mentioned it to her casually at breakfast.

It wasn't Mummy, Alva piped up, it was me. You? I said incredulously. Alva is not naturally tidy. Yes, I left them back after I'd borrowed them to wear over to Sarah's house. (Sarah is a friend of hers.) You what? You borrowed my boots, without even asking me? You went into my room and just took them? Alva nodded, her mouth full of toast. It was obvious from the way she had spoken that it hadn't even occurred to her that I would be annoyed. That made it worse, the way she took it for granted that my things were just there to be borrowed. How dare you! The cheek of you! I was shaking with rage. The thought of that little brat wandering into my room and just taking whatever took her fancy really got me worked up. Anyway, I said sarcastically, I thought they were too big for your dainty little feet.

No, not really, Alva said, trying to sound nonchalant. I was only teasing when I said that.

Only teasing, huh? I said, and I leant over the breakfast table and I told her, through clenched teeth, spitting the words out, that she was never, ever, to take another thing of mine, never, ever, to go into my room without my express permission. I am sure my face was purple with apoplexy. Don't you lay your rapacious little fingers on anything I own, anything! I shouted at her. (Even as I raged at her, I was rather proud of that word rapacious.) And *I* am *not* only teasing. I mean it, Alva.

And then I really let fly. It wasn't about the boots any more. It wasn't even about the invasion of my bedroom, it was about the whole thing, about Dad's betrayal of Mum, the pregnancy, the marriage, the throwing of us all together, the enforced sharing of this house, my house, our house, with these strangers, the sudden unwanted acquisition of steprelations I never asked for, Margaret's neurotic tidiness, the magnets on the fridge, the way Margaret took the apples off the neighbours' tree as if she owned it, owned the garden, owned Dad, even the way that she discussed making apple jelly with Robbie, as if she was just a normal, ordinary mother entertaining her daughter's boyfriend and making smalltalk, when she was anything, anything, *anything* but. I started roaring at Alva, really roaring, standing there in my school uniform with a slice of toast and marmalade in my hand. Do you understand, do you? do you? I had a pain in my chest. I realised afterwards I had hurt my lungs from screaming so loudly at Alva. And all the while she just sat there, chewing maddeningly, making my anger worse. She wasn't doing it on purpose, even in my rage I knew that, it had become a sort of mechanical action, brought on by horror at the way I was going on. I could hear Margaret's voice in the background, calling my father, telling him to get down here quick, his daughter was losing her reason. There were tears

in her voice, and panic, and there were tears pouring down Alva's face too, and still I couldn't stop roaring at her.

Then Ashling stood up – she was sitting next to Alva – and she leant over the breakfast things and caught hold of two handfuls of my hair, a bit like I had done to Emma O'Mara, except that my hair is longer and affords a much better grip, and she gave an almighty pull in opposite directions at once. It hurt like hell. I flung the toast out of my hand – it hit Alva in the face, but I didn't mean it to, I only realised it had landed on her nose afterwards – and put my two hands up and started to scratch the backs of Ashling's hands with my nails, shouting at her all the time Let go, Let go, Let go, you bitch. No, she shouted back at me, No, not until you promise to leave Alva alone. Leave her alone, leave her alone. All right, all right, but let GO! She did, abruptly taking her hands away. I saw through my tears – not tears of anger or tears of regret, just those tears your eyes fill up with when something really hurts hard – that the backs of her hands were badly scratched, long thin red lines on them, dotted with beads of blood. She started to suck them, as I nursed my head, and this was the scene that met Dad when he came into the kitchen (he's not first up any more). He sat down at the table and put his head in his hands, very effective, typical Dad. Margaret sat next to him and twisted a silk scarf she was wearing around and around and whispered, Girls, girls, oh girls. She really is a total wimp. I'm glad she's not my mother.

I stopped snivelling first. I'm sorry, Alva, I said, loudly, so they could all hear. I shouldn't have shouted at you like that, but you do see that you shouldn't have done it, don't you. Alva was crying loudly now, but she nodded. I am not Ashling, I said, you can't just take my things the way you would take hers. This is my home,

and I am entitled to privacy at least in my own room. I could feel the anger rising up in my throat again at this point. Then Ashling started. She said very quietly, Just shut up, will you Cindy. I could hardly believe my ears. What? I said. Shut UP, Cindy, she said more loudly, SHUT UP! We are all sick of you and your house and your things and *your* father and *your* bereavement and *your* bloody feelings, so will you please just shut up about it now, and forget it. It's only a pair of shoes, after all, and pretty horrible shoes too, if it comes to it.

You keep your opinions about my footwear to yourself, I snarled at her, and then I started shouting again. This time it was Dad who stopped me. He didn't pull my hair. He just put his hand over my mouth. I went on screaming and I tried to bite his hand, but he held firm, and eventually I stopped shouting and collapsed in fits of sobbing, beating my head off the kitchen table, and getting marmalade in my hair. By the time I surfaced, Ashling and Alva had left. I don't know if they had gone to school, or just gone to their room. Margaret was still there, looking very pale and washed out. I felt terrible, angry still, but guilty too and ashamed of my behaviour. It wasn't like tantrums I'd had, where I was in control. In this case, the storm had taken me over, instead of the other way around.

Here, said Dad, giving me a glass of water, a paper tissue and two white tablets. Take this, and then go to bed for an hour and sleep it off. I used the tissue, drank the water, but refused the tablets. I don't do drugs, I sniffed. Paracetamol is not drugs, shouted Dad. It is, I said sulkily, and there's no need to shout. Don't you talk to me about shouting, he said, but he lowered his voice. In fact, he sort of hissed it. He was very angry, which I think is a bit of a cheek, when you consider how charming *his* behaviour

has been through all of this. Then he told Margaret to go back to bed too. She was looking very pale and shaky, and I did feel a bit sorry for her, but there, it's partly her fault too, this is what happens when you go around breaking up people's homes. I'll ring the school, he said, and say you will both be in after break.

I lay in bed, but sleep wouldn't come. Usually if you have a good cry, you can slip off to sleep really easily afterwards, but this time, my head ached and pounded and I felt as if my brain was on fire. Maybe I should have taken the paracetamol after all.

I got up after an hour. My eyes were stinging, and there was a dull gong beating in my head. I washed my face with cold water. It was deliciously soothing to my puffy eyelids. Then I brushed my hair – that's when I discovered the marmalade – and went downstairs and sat quietly in the drawing room, waiting for Margaret.

Fights are supposed to be cathartic (that means it's tough going at the time, but it sort of cleanses and purifies you, a bit like Lent or Purgatory or Greek tragedy, I read it in an essay on Shakespeare – we do this pretty cool stuff in English this year). But in real life it doesn't seem to work that way. I don't feel a bit cleansed. I just feel worn out. I didn't know Ashling felt like that. I was quite shocked when she said all that about me. I thought maybe we could eventually get to be, well, not friends, but at least to tolerate each other, see the other one's point of view. But maybe it isn't really me she is so mad at. All that stuff about my bereavement, my feelings, I bet that is all coming from her mother, the stupid woman. She's such a *victim*, and she doesn't even know it.

For a little while there, it was nearly like being a family, though. It was certainly a family sort of fight. But it didn't last. We went back to being polite. Maybe that's the way it will go – we start

behaving like a family for a little while, and then we remember, and start being nice to each other again, and then gradually we will stop remembering and we will forget to be nice, and in the end we will all settle down into being a normalish sort of family – people who live together and row a lot. Maybe that's how families just are. Maybe it's not about playing charades and going to parent–teacher meetings. Maybe it's more about fighting over shoes and who gets to sit on the hump in the back seat. Or maybe it isn't and we won't.

Anyway, we all apologised to each other beautifully at dinner, everyone rushing in to say it had been their fault. Alva said it was all her fault for taking the boots, which really it was. But I said no, it was my fault, I'd over-reacted, which I didn't really believe, but I wasn't going to be outdone. And then Ashling said she'd spoken out of turn too, and she was sorry. And Margaret said she should have made sure Alva knew not to take my things, so really it was all her fault. Only Dad didn't join in the mass confession. I didn't notice at the time, but now I come to think of it, it was all really his fault, wasn't it? I mean, if he hadn't got Margaret pregnant, then none of this would have happened, they wouldn't have got married, Alva wouldn't have been here in the first place to borrow my Docs, so really it's all Dad's fault. It's all his fault, the whole miserable business. Oh Dad, why did you do this to me? It's all so horrible, I hate it. I want it to go back to being like it was before, even like it was after Mum died. At least then it was just you and me.

Friday 28th November

Of course, on the other hand, if all this had never happened, if Dad hadn't married Margaret, then I wouldn't have been at

Imelda's that night, and I would never have met Robbie. Was it worth it all to meet him? I wouldn't go that far, but he is pretty cool. Really he is. He's funny and kind and he's a great kisser. And he looks quite nice, too, sort of smiley and crinkly. Not as hand-some as Red Hugh, I have to say, but much more fun. It's nice to have a boyfriend, even if he isn't really. It's more than nice. It's rapid. I think I'll ring him in the morning.

Sunday 30th November

I went out with Robbie last night. I wore a jumper Ashling lent me. It was my first ever real proper date. I asked Dad if I could, and he said, Fine, fine, he seems a nice boy, but be home before eleven-thirty.

I thought he should have put up more of a fight. I thought fathers were supposed to say, Over my dead body, and Never darken my door again. Maybe he was just glad to get me out of the house for a while.

He didn't come on his motor bike, Robbie, I mean. He hasn't got one actually, it's Ger's that he goes on sometimes. He came on his push bike and he locked it to the drainpipe behind our house. Then we went into town on the bus. The lights were on in Henry Street, for Christmas. I don't like it being Christmassy too early, but it will be December tomorrow. It was lovely, like fairyland, and the air was sharp and cold and it made the lights seem to twinkle even more, and town was full of people, even though the shops were closed. We went to see a film in The Lighthouse, something in French, I think it was 18s, but I don't see why. It wasn't violent or dirty or anything, though it had some good sexy bits, but tasteful, you know. Anyway, I'm nearly six-teen. Afterwards we crossed the Ha'penny Bridge, holding hands

– I like holding hands, it's nearly the best part – and looked down into the river, the lights sparkling in the water, all wavery and shimmering. Then we skipped over the hump and raced across the road and into Merchant's Arch and we wandered through all the crowds in Temple Bar, it was like the middle of the day, except for the street lights.

Then we went for our bus because it was nearly a quarter to eleven. It was cold at the bus-stop and Robbie put his arms around me to keep me warm, and it was all snug in there, and I said, We're good at bus-stops, aren't we. He said we were great at bus-stops and gave me an extra-special hug and kissed the top of my head, and I felt safe and happy and I thought, this is great, this is what it's all about, this is how you grow up, this is what life after being a child is like, this is me, with someone I choose to be with, doing something I choose to do, not just missing Mum or hating Dad, being annoyed with Ashling or Alva, getting impatient with Margaret, thinking about the baby, this is just me, doing something for me, with somebody I really like, and it's great. Some day I will get to live that life all the time, have my own place, my own friends, control of my own life, choose who I live with and where I go, be like Imelda, free.

And then the bus came, and we got on it, and we trundled home.

You're not going to believe this. Alva just told me
Ashling keeps a diary too. I can't imagine what she
puts in it. Nothing ever seems to happen in her life.
I'd love to get hold of it, though, just to see what
Miss Prim thinks of me. She probably thinks
I'm quite nice, actually.